Neat Knitting Projects

A Permanent Reference Work for All Knitters.

By
Ruhama Weiner

Editor: *Ruth Benedict*
Layout and Design: *Keith Bush*
Photography: *Nick Patrinos*
Illustrations: *Jan Sanford*
Production: *Sally Radtke, Peggy Bjorkman, Tom Hunt,*
Greg Kot, Sue Des Rochers
Consulting Editor: *Mary Lamb Becker*

International Standard Book Number: 0-8467-0543-5
Library of Congress Catalog Card Number: 78-62697

A Word About This Book's Knitter

Behind every good knitter are good patterns, and good styles. And the woman who designed these patterns is one of the most creative, experienced knitters around.

FOR ALMOST 50 YEARS, Ruhama Weiner (at left) has been knitting, crocheting, embroidering, sewing and needlepointing as a hobby.

And for the past 15 years, she and her husband, Al, have turned this hobby into a business through the operation of "Ruhama's Yarn and Fabrics" shop. The Milwaukee, Wisconsin based shop has become well-known for its selection of materials, accessories, and friendly knitting advice.

But it's been much more than just service and materials that keep customers coming back time and time again. One of the reasons that knitters keep coming back is because they can choose from thousands of unique, beautiful needlecraft designs and patterns—each one an original created by Ruhama herself.

The All-Time Favorites. The 60 patterns displayed in this book are the all-time favorites of Ruhama's many customers. The patterns have been knit by every level of knitter from beginner to advanced—a fine commentary on the ease of understanding, performance and fit you'll find in all of them.

Three things that set this book apart from those of many other knitting designers' books are the perfect shape, hang, and durability you'll find in garments knit from these patterns. Ruhama's secret is that the designs—along with the many fitting tips given in this book—are based on fine sewing methods.

Knit 'Em Again and Again. This knitting book will hopefully find a place as a permanent reference book among your various yarns and knitting needles. No matter what styles you like or what yarns you use, you'll enjoy using these patterns again and again.

To get an entirely fresh look the second or third time you knit one of these patterns, simply switch to a different yarn. And you'll find patterns in this book for all ages—women, men, teenagers and young tots alike.

Happy Knitting!

─────CONTENTS─────

3

TOTS TO TEENS FASHIONS...

PLUS THESE EXTRAS...

How We Abbreviated Our Patterns

Knitting Terms:
k—knit
p—purl
oz—ounce(s)
dec—decrease, decreasing
inc—increase, increasing
beg—beginning
st(s)—stitch(es)
ss—stockinette stitch
psso—pass slip stitch over

yo—yarn over
sl—slip
tog—together
k 3b, k 2b, etc.—knit as many stitches
 shown in back loop of stitch
dp—double point
sp—single point
sl st—slip stitch
MC—Main Color
CC—Contrasting Color

rep—repeat, repeating
sk—skip
in(s)—inch, inches
SKP—skip 1, knit 1, and pass over
garter stitch—knit all rows and
 all stitches

Crocheting Terms:
ch—chain
sc—single crochet
dc—double crochet

All knitting directions contained in this book have been carefully checked by our staff for completeness and accuracy.
We cannot be responsible for typographical errors, misinterpretation of instructions or variance of individual knitters.

*Camping, biking, hiking—
the all seasons, all reasons sweater...*

Pullover Set-in Sleeve Sweater

Probably the most basic, most-knit sweater there is. This women's pattern turns out the same great looks as our tots and teens set-in pullover shown on page 66.

Yarn: Worsted Weight 16 (16-20-20) oz.
Blocked Measurement: 36 (38-40-42) inches for sweater at bust.
Gauge: In stockinette stitch (ss) 4½ stitches (sts) per inch.
Needles: Single point No. 6 and No. 9 or as needed to reach proper gauge. Double point No. 6.
Accessories: 2 st holders.

BACK

Cast on 80 (86-90-94) sts with small sp needles. Rib in k 1, p 1 for 2½ ins. Change to larger needles and continue in ss straight to 13 ins from the bottom of the ribbing. Blocked width 18 (19-20-21) ins.

Armhole: Bind off 4 (4-5-5) sts beg of next 2 rows. Dec 1 st every other row at each armhole edge 6 (7-7-7) times. Continue straight to 8½ (9-9½-10) ins from bind-off.

Shoulder: Bind off 7 sts beg of next 2 rows and 6 (7-7-8) sts beg of next 4 rows. Place the balance 22 (22-24-24) sts on a holder.

FRONT

Crew neck: Same as the back to 6 (6½-7-7½) ins above underarm. Place center 14 sts on a holder. Attach a 2nd ball of yarn so you can work each side of the neck at the same time. Dec 1 st at each neck edge every other row 4 (4-5-5) times. When the armhole measures the same as the back, bind off at each shoulder 7 sts 1 time, and 6 (7-7-8) sts 2 times.

V-neck: Same as back to underarm. Divide the sts evenly, attaching a 2nd ball of yarn so you can work both sides of neck at the same time. Dec 1 st at each neck edge every 5 rows 11 (11-12-12) times.

When armhole is same length as on back, bind off at each shoulder 7 sts 1 time and 6 (7-7-8) sts twice.

SLEEVES (Make 2)

Cast on 36 (38-40-42) sts using smaller needles. Rib in k 1, p 1 for 2½ ins. Change to larger needles and inc 4 sts evenly across row. Work in ss and inc 1 st each end of needle every 1 in until 60 (62-64-66) sts. Work straight to 17 (17½-18-18) ins from the bottom.

Armhole: Bind off 4 (4-5-5) sts beg of next 2 rows. Dec 1 st each end of needle every other row for 4¼ (4¾-5¼-5¾) ins. Bind off 2 sts beg of next 4 rows. Bind off balance.

Finishing: Sew shoulder seams, sleeve seams and side seams. Insert sleeves into armholes.

Crew neck: With right side facing you and using dp needles, pick up approximately 64 (64-66-68) sts around neck. Rib in k 1, p 1 for 1 in. Bind off *loosely in ribbing.*

V-neck: With right side facing you and using dp needles, pick up 22 (22-24-24) sts across back of neck and approximately 43 (46-48-50) sts on each front. Place a ring marker on the needle at the V. Rib in k 1, p 1 to 2 sts before the marker; k 2 tog, sl the marker, sl 1, k 1, psso; complete the round in k 1, p 1. Rep the round for 1 in. Bind off *loosely in ribbing.*

Knit-Picking...

Handmade or homemade?

The difference between a handmade knit and a homemade knit is in the way the garment is finished off. You'll find a number of helpful finishing tips like this scattered throughout this book.

Braided Beauty (see page 15)   **Cardigan Raglan Sleeve Sweater**

A fashion accent that's really versatile for all occasions…

Cardigan Raglan Sleeve Sweater

What's more popular and flattering than a raglan sleeve cardigan? Our sweater on the right is perfect over your shoulders when it's breezy outside, or worn as the final piece of your outfit.

Yarn: Worsted Weight 16 (20-20-20) oz.
Blocked Measurement: 36 (38-40-42) inches for sweater at bust.
Gauge: In stockinette stitch (ss) 4½ stitches (sts) per inch, 6 rows per inch,

Needles: Single point No. 6 and No. 9, or as needed to reach proper gauge.
Accessories: 3 st holders.

BACK

Cast on 80 (86-90-94) sts with smaller needle. Rib in k 1, p 1 for 2 ½ ins. Change to larger needles and continue in ss straight to 13 ins from the bottom of the ribbing. Blocked width: 18 (19-20-21) ins.

Armhole: Bind off 2 sts beg of next 2 rows. Work 2 rows even. Dec 1 st every other row at each armhole edge until 22 (22-22-24) sts remain. For crew neck, place on a holder. For V-neck, bind off.

RIGHT FRONT

Cast on 44 (46-50-52) sts with smaller needle. Rib in k 1, p 1 for 2½ ins. Keeping the center edge 6 sts in k 1, p 1 for the border, change to larger needles and continue in ss to 13 ins from the bottom of the ribbing.

Crew neck and armhole: Bind off 2 sts at armhole edge. Work 2 rows even. Dec 1 st at the same edge every other row as for the back. When the sweater measures 6¼ (6¾-7¼-7¾) ins above the underarm, start the neck.

Neckline: At the center edge place 10 (10-11-12) sts on a holder. Dec 1 st at the same edge every other row 5 (4-5-5) times. Continue raglan dec to 0 sts.

V-neck and armhole: Bind off 2 sts at the armhole edge. Work 2 rows even and dec raglan the same as on the back. *At the same time as the armhole is started, start the neck.* Do all neck dec just inside the 6 front border sts. Dec 1 st every 6 (7-6-6) rows 9 (8-10-11) times. When only the 6 border sts remain continue for another 2 ins. Bind off.

LEFT FRONT

Same as right front but *reverse shaping.* Rib in p 1, k 1.

SLEEVES (Make 2)

Cast on 36 (38-40-42) sts using smaller needles. Rib in k 1, p 1 for 2 ins. Change to larger needles and inc 4 sts evenly across row. Work in ss and inc 1 st each end of needle every 1¼ ins until 62 (64-66-68) sts. Continue straight to 17 (17½-18-18) ins from the bottom of the ribbing.

Armhole: Bind off 2 sts beg of next 2 rows. Work 2 (4-4-4) rows even. Dec 1 st each end of needle every other row until 2 sts remain. Bind off. Sew in sleeves. Sew side and sleeve seams.

Crew neck: With right side facing you and smaller needles, pick up 75 (77-79-81) sts around neck. Rib in k 1, p 1 for 1 in. Bind off loosely in ribbing.

V-neck: Sew the band together and attach it to the back of the sweater neck. Face each front edge with grosgrain ribbon. Make machine buttonholes and sew on buttons.

Be A Knit Whiz…

So tell me, how do I measure?

The age of a child, dress size, shirt size, arms held in the air all "sort of" show dimensions. But none of these methods will help you get the proper size for knitting.

So get a tape measure and follow these simple directions:

1. For young girls, boys and men: Measure the chest, at the underarm—both fully expanded and relaxed. If the garment is to be used for active sports, be sure to allow for the expanded chest measurement and movement. Add 2-4 inches to the chest measurement, depending on how your wearer likes a fit. The heavier the yarn, the more "ease" will be needed.

2. Developed girls and mature women: With a firm, but not overly tight tape, measure at the fullest part of the bust. Add 2-4 inches for ease, depending on the type of fit the wearer likes.

For very loose styles, such as the Lacey Blouson on p. 23, add 4-6 inches to the bust measurement. Then select the blocked measurement instructions in the pattern that come closest to the resulting total.

A traditional pattern with an "always-in-style" look…

Pullover Raglan Sleeve Sweater

This ever-popular sweater is always comfortable and just naturally great with everything from your wardrobe! Knit one in a crew neck or v-neck style.

Yarn: Worsted Weight 16 (20-20-20) oz.
Blocked Measurement: 36 (38-40-42) inches for sweater at bust.
Gauge: In stockinette stitch (ss) 4½ stitches (sts) per inch, 6 rows per inch.

Needles: Single point No. 6 and No. 9 or as needed to reach proper gauge. Double point No. 6.
Accessories: 2 st holders.

BACK

Cast on 80 (86-90-94) sts with smaller needles. Rib in k 1, p 1 for 2½ ins. Change to larger needles and continue in ss straight to 13 ins from the bottom. Blocked width 18 (19-20-21) ins.

Armhole: Bind off 2 sts beg of next 2 rows. Work 2 rows even. Dec 1 st every other row at each armhole edge until 22 (22-22-24) sts remain. Place on a holder.

FRONT

Crew neck: Same as back to 6¼ (6¾-7¼-7¾) ins above the underarm. Place center 12 (12-12-14) sts on a holder. Attach a 2nd ball of yarn so you can work both sides of neck at the same time. Dec 1 st at each neck edge 5 times. At the same time continue the raglan to 0 sts.

V-neck: Same as the back to the underarm. Divide the sts evenly; attach a 2nd ball of yarn and work both sides of neck at the same time. Work the armholes as on the back. Dec 1 st at each neck edge every 5 (5-6-5) rows 11 (11-11-12) times. Continue raglan dec to 0 sts.

SLEEVES (Make 2)

Cast on 38 (38-40-44) sts with the smaller needles. Rib in k 1, p 1 for 2½ ins. Change to larger needles and inc 4 sts evenly across row. Work in ss and inc 1 st each end of needle every 1¼ ins until 60 (64-66-70) sts. Continue straight to 17 (17½-18-18) ins from bottom.

Armhole: Bind off 2 sts beg of next 2 rows. Work 2 (4-4-4) rows even. Dec 1 st each end of needle every other row until 2 sts remain. Bind off.

Sew sleeves into body. Sew sleeve and side seams.

Crew neck: With right side facing you and smaller dp needles, pick up approximately 64 (64-64-68) sts around neck. Rib in k 1, p 1 for 1 in. Bind off *loosely* in ribbing.

V-neck: With right side facing you and smaller dp needles, pick up 22 (22-22-24) sts across back neck, and approximately 43 (46-48-50) sts on each front. Place a ring marker on needle at the V. Rib in k 1, p 1 to 2 sts before the marker; k 2 tog, sl the marker, sl 1, k 1, psso, complete the round in k 1, p 1. Rep this row for 1 in. Bind off loosely in ribbing.

Knit-Picking...

How do I knit the right size?

The patterns in this book were designed to reach the final "blocked measurement"—that is, the final dimensions of the finished sweater at the underarm, over the chest or bust.

Measure the wearer carefully, then add the proper amount of ease. Select the pattern size that gives you the closest number of inches at the chest. You may have to adjust lengths if the wearer is short or long in the body or arms.

Doing the duplicate stitch

When making duplicate stitches, be sure to work loosely so the top yarn covers the stitch adequately, as shown below.

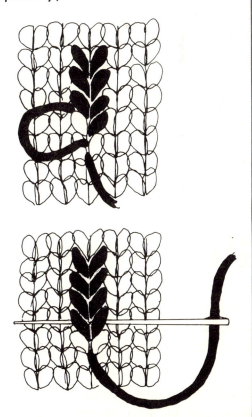

Neat and easy—a really fine basic for everything you own...

Cardigan Set-in Sleeve Sweater

This women's pattern makes a sweater with the same good looks as our men's classic set-in sleeve cardigan on page 42. Try different colors, buttons for a unique sweater look in crew or v-neck styles.

Yarn: Worsted Weight 16 (16-20-20) oz.
Blocked Measurement: 36 (38-40-42) inches for sweater at bust.
Gauge: In stockinette stitch (ss) 4½ stitches (sts) per inch.
Needles: Single point No. 6 and No. 9 or as needed to reach proper gauge.
Accessories: 3 st holders.

BACK

Cast on 80 (86-90-94) sts using smaller needle. Rib in k 1, p 1 for 2½ ins. Change to larger needles and continue in ss straight to 13 ins from the bottom of ribbing. Blocked measurement: 18 (19-20-21) ins across.

Armhole: Bind off 4 (4-5-5) sts beg of next 2 rows. Dec 1 st every other row at each armhole edge 6 (7-7-7) times. Continue straight to 8½ (9-9½-10) ins from bind off.

Shoulder: Bind off 7 sts beg of next 4 rows and 5 (6-7-9) sts beg of next 2 rows. For crew neck, place balance 22 (24-24-24) sts on a holder. For V-neck, bind off.

RIGHT FRONT

Cast on 44 (46-50-52) sts using smaller needles. Rib in k 1, p 1 for 2½ ins. Keeping center edge 6 sts in k 1, p 1 for the border, change to larger needles and continue in ss to 13 ins from the bottom of ribbing.

Crew neck and armhole: Bind off 4 (4-5-5) sts at armhole edge. Dec 1 st at same edge every other row 6 (7-7-7) times. Continue straight to 6 (6½-7-7½) ins. At center edge place 10 (11-12-12) sts on a holder. Dec 1 st at same edge every other row 5 (4-5-6) times. When armhole measures same as back, bind off at the shoulder edge 7 sts 2 times, and 5 (6-7-8) sts 1 time.

V-neck and armhole: Bind off 4 (4-5-5) sts at armhole edge. Work to last 8 sts, k 2 tog (neck dec), work border. Continue as established, doing all neck dec just inside the 6 border sts. Dec 1 st at the armhole edge every other row 6 (7-7-7) times, and at the same time dec at the neck edge 1 st every 6th row 8 (8-10-10) times more. When armhole measures the same as the back, bind off for shoulder 7 sts 2 times and 5 (6-7-9) sts 1 time. Continue the 6 border sts for another 2 ins. Bind off.

LEFT FRONT

Same as right front but *reverse shaping*. Rib in p 1, k 1.

SLEEVES (Make 2)

Cast on 38 (38-40-42) sts using smaller needles. Rib in k 1, p 1 for 2 ins. Change to larger needles and inc 4 sts evenly across row. Work in ss and inc 1 st each end of needle every 1¼ ins until 60 (62-64-66) sts. Continue straight to 17 (17½-18-18) ins from the bottom.

Armhole: Bind off 4 (4-5-5) sts beg of next 2 rows. Dec 1 st each end of needle every other row for 4½ (5-5½-5¾) ins. Bind off 2 sts beg of next 4 rows. Bind off balance.

FINISHING

Sew shoulder seams, sleeve seams and side seams. Insert sleeves into armholes.

Crew neck: With right side facing you and using smaller needles, pick up 75 (77-79-81) sts around neck. Rib in k 1, p 1 for 1 in. Bind off *loosely in ribbing.*

V-neck: Sew band together and attach to the back neck of sweater. Face the fronts as desired with preshrunk grosgrain ribbon and make machine buttonholes. Sew on buttons.

Try a truly feminine look with this pretty, lacy cardigan...

Autumn Haze

An imaginative little lace-like sweater, with zig-zag designs up and down the front. It's perfect for intermediate knitters, plus soft and dressy. Shown on page 62.

Yarn: Knitting Worsted Weight 16 (20-20-24) oz.

Blocked Measurement: 36 (38-40-42) inches for sweater at bust.

Gauge: In stockinette stitch (ss) 5 stitches (sts) per inch.

Needles: Single point No. 3 and No. 6 or as needed to reach proper gauge.

BACK

Cast on 90 (94-100-104) sts using smaller needle. Rib in k 1, p 1, for 1½ ins inc 1 st at end of last row. Change to larger needles and continue in following pattern until 12 ins from bottom of ribbing.

Row 1: Wrong side: P 28 (30-33-35), k 1, yarn forward, sl 1 as to p, p 2, k 2, sl 1, p 2, k 1, p 15, k 1, sl 1, p 2, k 2, sl 1, p 2, k 1, p 28 (30-33-35).

Row 2: K 28 (30-33-35), p 1, yarn back, insert needle into sl st of previous row (3rd st on left needle) as to k, k this st through front of st but do not drop from needle, k the first of the sk sts and remove it, sl the next st to the right needle and drop the next st from the left needle (sl st of previous row)—this is a right cross (RC)—p 2, RC, p 1, k 1, yo, sl 1, k 1, psso, k 2, yo, sl 1 k 1 psso, k 1, k 2 tog, yo, k 2, k 2 tog, yo, k 1, p 1, RC, p 2, RC, p 1, k 28 (30-33-35).

Row 3: And all odd rows: Same as row 1.

Row 4: K 28 (30-33-35), p 1, RC, p 2, RC, p 1, k 2, yo, sl 1 k 1 psso, k 2, yo, sl 1, k 2 tog, psso, yo, k 2, k 2 tog, yo, k 2, p 1, RC, p 2, RC, p 1, k 28 (30-33-35).

Row 6: K 28 (30-33-35), p 1, RC, p 2, RC, p 1, k 3, yo, sl 1 k 1 psso, k 1, k 2 tog, yo, k 2, k 2 tog, yo, k 3, p 1, RC, p 2, RC,

p 1, k 28 (30-33-35).

Row 8: K 28 (30-33-35), p 1, RC, p 2, RC, p 1, k 4, yo, sl 1, k 2 tog, psso, yo, k 2, k 2 tog, yo, k 4, p 1, RC, p 2, RC, p 1, k 28 (30-33-35).

Row 10: K 28 (30-33-35), p 1, RC, p 2, RC, p 1, k 4, k 2 tog, yo, k 2, k 2 tog, yo, k 5, p 1, RC, p 2, RC, p 1, k 28 (30-33-35).

Row 12: K 28 (30-33-35), p 1, RC, p 2, RC, p 1, k 3, k 2 tog, yo, k 2, k 2 tog, yo, k 1, yo, sl 1 k 1 psso, k 3, p 1, RC, p 2, RC, p 1, k 28 (30-33-35).

Row 14: K 28 (30-33-35), p 1, RC, p 2, RC, p 1, k 2, k 2 tog, yo, k 2, k 2 tog, yo, k 3, yo, sl 1 k 1 psso, k 2, p 1, RC, p 2, RC, p 1, k 28 (30-33-35).

Row 16: K 28 (30-33-35), p 1, RC, p 2, RC, p 1, k 1, k 2 tog, yo, k 2, k 2 tog, yo, k 1, yo, sl 1, k 1 psso, k 2, yo, sl 1 k 1 psso, k 1, p 1, RC, p 2, RC, p 1, k 28 (30-33-35).

Row 18: K 28 (30-33-35), p 1, RC, p 2, RC, p 1, k 2 tog, yo, k 2, k 2 tog, yo, k 3, yo, sl 1, k 1 psso, k 2, yo, sl 1, k 1 psso, p 1, RC, p 2, RC, p 1, k 28 (30-33-35).

Rep above 18 rows for pattern until 12 ins from bottom of ribbing.

Armhole: Bind off 5 sts beg of next 2 rows. Dec 1 st every other row at each armhole edge 6 (7-8-9) times. Continue straight to 8¾ (9¼-9¾-10¼) ins from underarm.

Shoulder: Bind off 7 (7-8-8) sts beg of next 4 rows, and 8 sts beg of next 2 rows. Place balance 25 (27-27-29) sts on holder.

RIGHT FRONT

Cast on 50 (52-56-58) sts using smaller needles. Rib in k 1, p 1 for 1½ ins. Change to larger needles and continue in following pattern:

Row 1: (Wrong side) P 12 (14-18-20), *k 1, sl 1, p 2, k 2, sl 1, p 2, k 1, p 7, k 1, sl 1, p 2, k 2, sl 1, p 2, k 1*, p 3, rib 8.

Row 2: Rib 8, k 3, *p 1, RC, p 2, RC, p 1, k 1, yo, sl 1, k 1 psso, k 4, p 1, RC, p 2, RC, p 1*, k 12 (14-18-20).

Row 3: And all odd rows same as row 1.

Row 4: Rib 8, k 3, *p 1, RC, p 2, RC, p 1, k 2,

CONTINUED ON NEXT PAGE

CONTINUED FROM PREVIOUS PAGE

yo, sl 1 k 1 psso, k 3, p 1, RC, p 2, RC, p 1*, k 12 (14-18-20).

Row 6: Rib 8, k 3, *p 1, RC, p 2, RC, p 1, k 3, yo, sl 1 k 1 psso, k 2, p 1, RC, p 2, RC, p 1*, k 12 (14-18-20).

Row 8: Rib 8, k 3, *p 1, RC, p 2, RC, p 1, k 4, yo, sl 1 k 1 psso, k 1, p 1, RC, p 2, RC, p 1*, k 12 (14-18-20).

Row 10: Rib 8, k 3, *p 1, RC, p 2, RC, p 1, k 4, k 2 tog, yo, k 1, p 1, RC, p 2, RC, p 1*, k 12 (14-18-20).

Row 12: Rib 8, k 3, *p 1, RC, p 2, RC, p 1, k 3, k 2 tog, yo, k 2, p 1, RC, p 2, RC, p 1*, k 12 (14-18-20).

Row 14: Rib 8, k 3, *p 1, RC, p 2, RC, p 1, k 2, k 2 tog, yo, k 3, p 1, RC, p 2, RC, p 1*, k 12 (14-18-20).

Row 16: Rib 8, k 3, *p 1, RC, p 2, RC, p 1, k 1, k 2 tog, yo, k 4, p 1, RC, p 2, RC, p 1*, k 12 (14-18-20).

Row 18: Rib 8, k 3, *p 1, RC, p 2, RC, p 1, k 2 tog, yo, k 5, p 1, RC, p 2, RC, p 1*, k 12 (14-18-20).

Rep these 18 rows until 12 ins from bottom of ribbing. Start armhole.

Armhole: Bind off 5 sts at armhole edge. Dec 1 st at same edge every other row 6 (7-8-9) times. Continue straight to 6¼ (6¾-7¼-7¾) ins from underarm. Start neck: At front edge, place 12 (13-14-15) sts on a holder. Dec 1 st at same edge every other row 5 times. When armhole measures same as on back, bind off at shoulder edge 7 (7-8-8) sts 2 times and 8 sts 1 time.

LEFT FRONT
Same as right front but reverse shaping. Rib in p 1,

k 1. To reverse the pattern for left front, proceed this way: On first row after ribbing:

Row 1: Wrong side: Rib 8, p 3, rep between * of right front for next 27 sts, p 12 (14-18-20).

Row 2: K 12 (14-18-20), rep between * of right front for next 27 sts, k 3, rib 8.

Continue this way in an established pattern forming the balance of the front in reverse of right front. Be sure to reverse shaping.

SLEEVES (Make 2)
Cast on 38 (42-42-44) sts using smaller needles. Rib in k 1, p 1 for 2 ins. Change to larger needles inc 4 sts evenly across row. Work in ss and inc 1 st each end of needle every 1¼ ins until 64 (68-70-74) sts. Continue straight until 17 (17½-18-18) ins from bottom of ribbing.

Armhole: Bind off 5 sts beg of next 2 rows. Dec 1 st each end of needle every other row for 4½ (5-5½-6) ins. Bind off 2 sts beg of next 4 rows. Bind off balance.

FINISHING
Sew shoulder seams.

Neckline: With right side facing you and using smaller needles, pick up approximately 83 (85-87-89) sts around neck including sts on holders. Rib in k 1, p 1 for 2 ins. Bind off *loosely* in ribbing.

Sew side seams and sleeve seams. Insert sleeves into body. Block to size. Face fronts with grosgrain ribbon. Make machine buttonholes. Fold the neck band in half to the inside and tack down. Then, sew on buttons.

A perfect wardrobe extra for spring, fall or cool summer nights…

Cabled Swagger Jacket

Here's the women's fashion basic shown on the cover. Just right for casual and slightly dressier garments too!

Yarn: Knitting Worsted Weight 6 (7-8-8) oz.

Blocked Measurement: 36 (38-40-42) inches for sweater at bust.
Gauge: In stockinette stitch (ss) 5 stitches (sts) per inch, 7 rows per inch.
Needles: Single point No. 8, single point No. 6, 29 inch No. 6 circular needle, or as needed to reach proper gauge.
Accessories: Size H crochet needle.

BACK

Using larger needle, cast on 98 (104-110-114) sts. Continue this way for each particular size:

Sizes 36 (38)
Row 1: K 2 (5), *p 1, k 3, p 1, k 4, p 1, k 3, p 1, k 6, rep from * to last 16 (19) sts, end p 1, k 3, p 1, k 4, p 1, k 3, p 1, k 2 (5).
Rows 2, 4, 6, 8: Work sts as you see them.
Rows 3, 5, 7: Same as row 1.
Row 9: K 2 (5), *p 1, k 3, p 1, k 4, p 1, k 3, p 1, sl next 3 sts to cable holder and hold in back, k next 3 sts, k 3 from holder (cable turn made), rep from * to last 16 (19) sts, end p 1, k 3, p 1, k 4, p 1, k 3, p 1, k 2 (5).
Rep rows 2 through 9 for pattern.

Sizes 40 (42)
Row 1: K 1 (3), p 1 *k 6, p 1, k 3, p 1, k 4, p 1, k 3, p 1, rep from * to last 8 (10) sts, end k 6, p 1, k 1 (3).
Rows, 2, 4, 6, 8: Work sts as you see them.
Rows 3, 5, 7: Same as row 1.
Row 9: K 1 (3), p 1, *sl next 3 sts to cable holder and hold in back, k next 3 sts, k 3 from cable holder (cable turn made), p 1, k 3, p 1, k 4, p 1, k 3, p 1, rep from * to last 8 (10) sts, end with cable turn, p 1, k 1 (3).
Rep rows 2 through 9 for pattern.

All sizes: Work cable pattern to 17 ins from bottom. End so that next row is a right side row.

Armhole: Bind off 2 sts beg of next 2 rows. Keep cable pattern as established. Work 4 (2-2-0) rows even. Next row: K 3, sl 1, k 1, psso, work pattern st to last 5 sts, k 2 tog, k 3 (raglan dec row). Next row: Work sts as you see them.

Rep above two rows for raglan dec until 26 (28-30-32) sts remain. Bind off.

LEFT FRONT

Using larger needle, cast on 49 (52-55-57) sts. Establish cable pattern as follows:

Sizes 36 (38)
Row 1: K 2 (5), *p 1, k 3, p 1, k 4, p 1, k 3, p 1, k 6, rep from * one time, end p 1, k 3, p 1, k 2. Continue in cable pattern same as on back.

Sizes 40 (42)
Row 1: K 1 (3), p 1, *k 6, p 1, k 3, p 1, k 4, p 1, k 3, p 1, rep from * one more time, end k 6, p 1, k 3, p 1, k 2. Continue in cable pattern as on back.

All sizes: At 17 ins from bottom, end so you can start on k side for *left* front.

Armhole: Bind off 2 (2-2-3) sts. Work in pattern to end of row. Next row: K 2 tog (neck dec), continue working in cable pattern, work next 3 (1-3-1) rows

even, continue with raglan dec as on back while rep neck dec every 6th row 10 (11-12-13) times more. When 2 sts remain, fasten off.

RIGHT FRONT

Same as left front but reverse shaping and pattern placement. At underarm, bind off on the p side. Work 4 (2-2-0) rows even before starting the raglan dec.

SLEEVES (Make 2)

Using larger needle, cast on 46 (50-50-52) sts. Continue this way to establish cable pattern:

Size 36: P 1, k 4, p 1, k 3, p 1, k 6, p 1, k 3, p 1, k 4, p 1, k 3, p 1, k 6, p 1, k 3, p 1, k 4, p 1.

Sizes 38 (40-42): K 2 (2-3), p 1, k 4, p 1, k 3, p 1, k 6, p 1, k 3, p 1, k 4, p 1, k 3, p 1, k 6, p 1, k 3, p 1, k 4, p 1, k 2 (2-3).

With cable pattern established, work cable as on back inc 1 st at each end of needle every 8 rows to 72 (74-76-78) sts. Work inc sts into cable pattern. When sleeve measures 17½ (18-18-18) ins from bottom of sleeve, begin *armhole:* Bind off 2 sts beg of next 2 rows. Work 4 rows even. Continue raglan dec as on back until 2 sts remain. Fasten off.

COLLAR

With circular needle, cast on 324 (328-334-336) sts. Work back and forth in k 2, p 2 for 14 rows. Bind off 80 sts beg of next 2 rows, 3 sts beg of next 12 (12-14-14) rows, 9 sts beg of next 4 rows, 10 sts beg of next 4 rows, 13 sts beg of next 2 rows. Bind off balance of 26 (30-30-32) sts.

POCKET (Make 2)

Using short No. 6 needles, cast on 38 sts. Work in k 2, p 2 for 7 ins. Bind off.

BELT

Using smaller needle, cast on 20 sts. Work as follows: *K 1, yarn forward, sl 1 as to p, rep from * across row. Work all rows the same. Make belt 50 ins long or as desired. Bind off.

FINISHING

Attach sleeves. Sew side and sleeve seams. Attach collar, matching centers, and using collar's bound-off edge for seam. Attach collar ends to bottom edges of jacket. Where collar width increases, tack down at jacket V-neck dec. Complete sewing, with ease. Place pockets on front. Make belt loops in sc.

Discover the joy of soft, cuddly sweater knits…

Cable-Raglan Cardigan

The special fitting ease of the raglan style, yet with a better fit than most cable raglans knit on circular needles. Let yourself go with an exciting bright color or a delicate watercolor pastel.

Yarn: Sportsweight 12 (14-14) oz.
Blocked Measurement: 36 (38-40) inches for sweater at bust.
Gauge: In stockinette stitch (ss) 6 stitches (sts) per inch, 8 rows per inch.
Needles: Single point No. 3 and No. 5, or as needed for gauge. Double point No. 3.
Accessories: St holders.

BACK

Cast on 108 (114-120) on smaller needle. Rib in k 1, p 1 for 1½ ins. Change to larger needles. Continue in ss to 12 ins from bottom of ribbing.

Armhole Raglan Dec Pattern:

Row 1:   Bind off 2 sts, k 6, p 2, k to end of row.
Row 2:   Bind off 2 sts, p 6, k 2, p to last 9 sts, k 2, p 6, k 1.
Row 3:   P 1, k 6, p 2, sl 1, k 1, psso, k to last 11 sts, k 2 tog, p 2, k 6, p 1.
Row 4:   K 1, p 6, k 2, p to last 9 sts, k 2, p 6, k 1.
Row 5:   P 1, sl next 3 sts to dp needle and hold in back. K next 3 sts, k 3 sts from dp needle (cable turn), p 2 sl 1, k 1, psso, k to last 11 sts, k 2 tog, p 2, cable turn, p 1.

Rows 6, 8, 10, 12: Same as row 4.
Rows 7, 9, 11: Same as row 3.

Rep rows 5 through 12 for cable raglan until 30 (30-32) sts are left. Place on holder.

RIGHT FRONT

Cast on 62 (64-68) sts with smaller needles.

Row 1:   K 8, rib 54 (56-60).
Row 2:   Rib 54 (56-60), p 8.

Rep these 2 rows for 1½ ins. Change to larger needles and continue in ss, keeping 9 sts at front edge in k 8, p 1 for front band. When 12 ins from bottom of ribbing, start armhole.

Armhole Raglan Dec Pattern:

Row 1:   Bind off 2 sts at armhole edge, p 6, k 2, complete row.
Row 2:   Work to last 11 sts, k 2 tog, p 2, k 6, p 1.
Row 3:   K 1, p 6, k 2, work to end.
Rows 5, 7, 9, 11, 13: Same as row 3.
Rows 6, 8, 10, 12: Same as row 2.

Rep rows 4-13 for cable raglan until piece measures 6¼ (6¾-7¼) ins above underarm bind-off. Start neckline.

Neckline: Place 15 (15-16) sts at front edge on a holder. Dec 1 st at same edge every other row 6 (5-6) times. Maintain cable raglan pattern at armhole edge at same time. When raglan dec interfere with cable panel, stop cabling, keeping k and p sts in pattern as long as possible. Transfer raglan dec to armhole edge. Continue until 2 sts remain. Bind off.

LEFT FRONT

Same as right front but reverse shaping. Rib in k 1, p 1. Fashion armhole dec as on right side of back.

SLEEVES (Make 2)

Cast on 48 sts using smaller needles. Rib in k 1, p 1 for 2 ins. Change to larger needles and inc 6 sts evenly across row. Continue in ss inc 1 st each end of needle every 1 in until 76 (80-84) sts. Continue straight to 17½ (18-18) ins from bottom of ribbing.

Armhole:

Row 1:   Bind off 2 sts, p 2, k to end of row.
Row 2:   Bind off 2 sts, k 2, p to last 3 sts, k 3.
Rows 3 and 5: P 3, k to last 3 sts, p 3.
Rows 4 and 6: K 3, p to last 3 sts, k 3.
Row 7:   P 3, sl 1, k 1, psso, k to last 5 sts, k 2 tog, p 3.
Row 8:   Same as row 4.

Rep rows 7 and 8 until 2 sts are left. Bind off.

FINISHING

Sew in sleeves. With right side facing you and using smaller needles, pick up approximately 101 (101-103) sts. Form neckline:

Row 1:   P 8, rib k 1, p 1 to last 9 sts, k 1, p 8.
Row 2:   K 8, rib to last 8 sts, k 8.

Rep these 2 rows for 2 ins. Bind off loosely in ribbing.

Sew in sleeve and underarm seams. Block to size. Face fronts with grosgrain ribbon. Make machine buttonholes. Turn neck ribbing in half to inside and tack in place.

Come alive with lively braids...

Braided Beauty

Continuous braids run through ribbing on our smart cardigan on page 6.

Yarn: Sportsweight 12 (14-14) oz.
Blocked Measurement: 36 (38-40) inches for sweater at bust.
Gauge: In stockinette stitch (ss) 6 stitches (sts) per inch, 8 rows per inch.

CONTINUED ON NEXT PAGE

CONTINUED FROM PREVIOUS PAGE

Needles: Single point No. 3 and No. 5 or as needed to reach proper gauge. Cable needle.

Accessories: 3 st holders.

BACK

Cast on 109 (115-121) sts using smaller needles. Rib in pattern given below for 2 ins:

Row 1: (K 1, p 1) for 25 (27-29) sts, p 2, k 12, p 2, (k 1, p 1) for 27 (29-31) sts, p 2, k 12, p 2, (k 1, p 1) for 25 (27-29) sts.

Row 2: (P 1, k 1) for 25 (27-29) sts, k 2, p 12, k 2, (p 1, k 1) for 27 (29-31) sts, k 2, p 12, k 2, (p 1, k 1) for 25 (27-29) sts.

Row 3: (K 1, p 1) for 25 (27-29) sts, p 2, sl next 4 sts to a dp needle and hold in back. K next 4 sts, k 4 from dp needle, k next 4 sts (this is a back cable turn), p 2, (k 1, p 1) for 27 (29-31) sts, p 2, back cable turn, p 2, (k 1, p 1) for 25 (27-29) sts.

Rows 4, 6, 8: Same as row 2.

Rows 5, 7: Same as row 1.

Row 9: (K 1, p 1) for 25 (27-29) sts, p 2, k 4 sts, sl next 4 sts to a dp needle and hold in front, k next 4 sts, k 4 from dp needle (this is front cable turn), p 2, (k 1, p 1) for 27 (29-31) sts, p 2, front cable turn, p 2, (k 1, p 1) for 25 (27-29) sts.

Rows 10, 12, 14: Same as row 2.

Rows 11, 13: Same as row 1.

Rep rows 3-14, working pattern for 2 ins. End facing right side row. Change needles to larger size. K and inc 5 sts evenly across first 25 (27-29) sts, work 16 sts of cable panel, k and inc 5 sts evenly across next 27 (29-31) sts, work 16 sts of cable panel, k and inc 5 sts evenly across next 25 (27-29) sts. Continue this way working cable panels according to above pattern and keeping all other sts in ss until 12 ins from bottom of ribbing.

Armhole: Bind off 7 (8-8) sts beg of next 2 rows. Dec 1 st every face row at each armhole edge until 34 (34-36) sts are left. Place on holder.

RIGHT FRONT

Cast on 60 (62-66) sts using smaller needle. Rib in pattern given below for 2 ins:

Row 1: K 9, p 1, (k 1, p 1) for 9 (9-11) sts, p 2, k 12, p 2, (k 1, p 1) for 25 (27-29) sts.

Row 2: (P 1, k 1) for 25 (27-29) sts, k 2, p 12, k 2, (p 1, k 1) for 9 (9-11) sts, k 1, p 9.

Row 3: K 9, p 1, (k 1, p 1) for 9 (9-11) sts, p 2, back cable turn, p 2, (k 1, p 1) for 25 (27-29) sts.

Rows 4, 6, 8: Same as row 2.

Rows 5, 7: Same as row 1.

Row 9: K 9, p 1, (k 1, p 1) for 9 (9-11) sts, p 2, front cable turn, p 2, (k 1, p 1) for 25 (27-29) sts.

Rows 10, 12, 14: Same as row 2.

Rows 11, 13: Same as row 1.

Rep rows 3-14, working pattern for 2 ins. End facing a k row. Change to larger needles. K 9, p 1, inc 2 sts across next 9 (9-11) sts, work cable panel over next 16 sts, k and inc 5 sts evenly across next 25 (27-29) sts. Continue the 10 sts of front band and cable panel as established, work all other sts in ss. Continue straight to 12 ins from bottom of ribbing.

Armhole: Bind off 7 (8-8) sts at armhole edge. Dec 1 st at armhole edge every face row as on back. When piece measures 6¼ (6¾-7¼) ins from underarm, start neck.

Neckline: At front edge, place 14 (13-15) sts on holder. Dec 1 st at each neck edge, every face row 6 times. At same time continue raglan dec until 2 sts. Bind off.

LEFT FRONT

Same as right front except reverse order of pattern and shaping.

SLEEVES (Make 2)

Cast on 46 sts on smaller needles. Rib in pattern for 2 ins as follows:

Row 1: (K 1, p 1) for 15 sts, p 2, k 12, p 2, (k 1, p 1) for 15 sts.

Row 2: (P 1, k 1) for 15 sts, k 2, p 12, k 2, (p 1, k 1) for 15 sts.

Row 3: (K 1, p 1) for 15 sts, p 2, back cable turn, p 2, (k 1, p 1) for 15 sts.

Continue in rib and cable pattern as with rest of sweater. End at 2 ins facing right side row. Change to larger needles. K and inc 7 (7-8) sts across first 15 sts, work cable panel, k and inc 7 (7-8) sts across last 15 sts. Continue in ss and cable panel, inc 1 st each end of needle every 1 in until 84 (88-90) sts. Continue straight to 17½ (18-18) ins from bottom of ribbing.

Armhole: Bind off 6 sts beg of next 2 rows. Dec 1 st at each end of needle every 4th row 3 times, then every other row until 2 sts remain. Bind off.

Neckline: Sew sleeves into body. With right side facing you, and using smaller needle, pick up 105 (105-109) sts around neck. Next row, p 9, (k 1, p 1) rib over next 89 (89-93) sts, p last 9. Next row, k 9, p 1 rib to last 9 sts, k 9. Rep these 2 rows for ¾ in. Bind off loosely.

FINISHING

Sew side and sleeve seams. Block. Face front edges with preshrunk grosgrain ribbon. Make machine buttonholes. Sew on buttons.

Make a cheery impression with another lacy sweater look...

Lace-'N'-Cable Cardigan

A "go-with-everything separate" (next page) with enough variation to make it fun for expert knitters, yet simple enough for intermediates. A pretty cable decorates the back while lace panels trim the front.

Yarn: Sportsweight 12 (12-14-14) oz.
Blocked Measurement: 34 (36-38-40) inches for sweater at bust.
Gauge: In stockinette stitch (ss) 6 stitches (sts) per inch.
Needles: Single point No. 3 and No. 5 or as needed to reach proper gauge. Cable needle.
Accessories: St holders.

BACK
Cast on 102 (108-114-120) sts using smaller needles. Rib in k 1, p 1 for 2 ins. Change to larger needles. Continue in following pattern st:
Row 1:   K 31 (34-37-40), p 2, k 1, yo, sl 1 (as to p), k 1 psso, k 3, k 2 tog, yo, k 1, p 2, k 1, p 2, k 8, p 2, k 1, p 2, k 1, yo, sl 1, k 1 psso, k 3, k 2 tog, yo, k 1, p 2, k 31 (34-37-40).
Row 2:   *And all even rows:* P 31 (34-37-40), k 2, p 9, k 5, p 8, k 5, p 9, k 2, p 31 (34-37-40).
Row 3:   K 31 (34-37-40), p 2, k 2, yo, sl 1, k 1, psso, k 1, k 2 tog, yo, k 2, p 2, k 1, p 2, k 8, p 2, k 1, p 2, k 2, yo, sl 1, k 1, psso, k 1, k 2 tog, yo, k 2, p 2, k 31 (34-37-40).
Row 5:   K 31 (34-37-40), p 2, k 3, yo, sl 1, k 2 tog, psso, yo, k 3, p 2, k 1, p 2, k 8, p 2, k 1, p 2, k 3, yo, sl 1, k 2 tog, psso, yo, k 3, p 2, k 31 (34-37-40).
Row 7:   K 31 (34-37-40), p 2, k 2, k 2 tog, yo, k 1, yo, sl 1, k 1, psso, k 2, p 2, k 1, p 2, sl next 4 sts to a cable needle and hold in back, k 4, k 4 from cable needle, p 2, k 1, p 2, k 2, k 2 tog, yo, k 1, yo, sl 1, k 1, psso, k 2, p 2, k 31 (34-37-40).
Row 9:   K 31 (34-37-40), p 2, k 1, k 2 tog, yo, k 3, yo, sl 1, k 1, psso, k 1, p 2, k 1, p 2, k 8, p 2, k 1, p 2, k 1, k 2 tog, yo, k 3, yo, sl 1, k 1, psso, k 1, p 2, k 31 (34-37-40).

Row 11:   K 31 (34-37-40), p 2, sl 1, k 1, psso, yo, k 5, yo, sl 1, k 1, psso, p 2, k 1, p 2, k 8, p 2, k 1, p 2, sl 1, k 1, psso, yo, k 5, yo, sl 1, k 1, psso, p 2, k 31 (34-37-40).
Row 12:   Same as row 2.
Rep these 12 rows for pattern. When piece measures 13 ins from bottom of ribbing, start armhole. Check width to fit: 17 (18-19-20) ins.

Armhole: Bind off 7 sts beg of next 2 rows. Dec 1 st every other row at each armhole edge 7 (7-7-8) times. Continue straight to 8¼ (8¾-9¼-9¾) ins from bind off.

Shoulder: Bind off 6 (6-7-7) sts beg of next 6 rows and 5 (7-7-8) sts beg of next 2 rows. Place balance of 28 (30-30-32) sts on a holder.

RIGHT FRONT
Cast on 58 (60-62-66) sts using smaller needle. Rib in k 1, p 1 for 2 ins. Change to larger needles. Continue in following pattern st:
Row 1:   (K 1, p 1) for 10 sts, k 12 (13-14-16), p 2, k 1, yo, sl 1 k 1 psso, k 3, k 2 tog, yo, k 1, p 2, k 23 (24-25-27).
Row 2:   *And all even rows:* P 23 (24-25-27), k 2, p 9, k 2, p 12 (13-14-16), (k 1, p 1) for 10 sts.
Row 3:   (K 1, p 1) 10 sts, p 12 (13-14-16), p 2, k 2, yo, sl 1 k 1 psso, k 1, k 2 tog, yo, k 2, p 2, k 23 (24-25-27).
Row 5:   (K 1, p 1) 10 sts, k 12 (13-14-16), p 2, k 3, yo, sl 1, k 2 tog, psso, yo, k 3, p 2, k 23 (24-25-27).
Row 7:   (K 1, p 1) 10 sts, k 12 (13-14-16), p 2, k 2, k 2 tog, yo, k 1, yo, sl 1, k 1, psso, k 2, p 2, k 23 (24-25-27).
Row 9:   (K 1, p 1) 10 sts, k 12 (13-14-16), p 2, k 1, k 2 tog, yo, k 3, yo, sl 1 k 1 psso, k 1, p 2, k 23 (24-25-27).
Row 11:   (K 1, p 1) 10 sts, k 12 (13-14-16), p 2, sl 1 k 1 psso, yo, k 5, yo, sl 1 k 1 psso, p 2, k 23 (24-25-27).
Row 12:   Same as row 2.
Rep these 12 rows for pattern. When piece measures 13 ins from bottom of ribbing, start underarm. Check width for fit: 9½ (10-10½-11) ins.

CONTINUED ON NEXT PAGE

CONTINUED ON NEXT PAGE

CONTINUED FROM PAGE 17

Armhole: Bind off 7 sts at armhole edge. Dec 1 st at armhole edge every other row 7 (7-7-8) times maintaining pattern as established. Continue straight to 5¾ (6¼-6¾-7¼) ins from bind-off. Start neck: At front edge place 15 (15-15-16) sts on a holder. Dec 1 st at same edge every other row 6 (6-5-6) times. When armhole measures same as back, bind off at shoulder edge 6 (6-7-7) sts 3 times and 5 (7-7-8) sts 1 time.

LEFT FRONT

Same as right front but reverse shaping. Rib in p 1, k 1.

SLEEVES (Make 2)

Cast on 44 (46-48-50) sts using smaller needles. Rib in k 1, p 1 for 2 ins. Change to larger needles, inc 6 sts evenly across row. Work in ss inc 1 st at each end of needle every 1 in until 74 (76-80-82) sts on needle. Check width: Approximately 12¼ (12¾-13¾-13¾) ins. Continue straight to 17 (17-18-18) ins from bottom of ribbing.

Armhole: Bind off 7 sts beg of next 2 rows. Dec 1 st at each end of needle every other row for 4 (4½-5-5½) ins. Bind off 2 sts beg of next 4 rows. Bind off balance.

FINISHING

Sew shoulder seams.

Neckline: With right side facing you and using smaller needles, pick up 99 (101-101-103) sts around neck. Rib in k 1, p 1 for 2 ins. Bind off *loosely* in ribbing.

Sew sleeve and side seams. Insert sleeves into sweater. Block. Back front edges of cardigan with preshrunk grosgrain ribbon. Turn neck in half to inside and tack down. Make machine buttonholes. Sew on buttons.

Be A Knit Whiz...

Picking up an edge

Mark off the area to be picked up (front band, neck, etc.) with stainless steel T-pins, dividing the piece in half, and then in half again. Repeat until you have several sections of a workable size—perhaps an inch or two in a span. Count the number of stitches to be picked up and divide them evenly into the number of sections.

If there are extra stitches, divide them evenly among the sections.

You'll need a crochet hook small enough to work into the edge of the garment, a knitting needle for picked up stitches, and a ball of yarn.

Remember: NEVER take a stitch that's been previously knit, and simply slip it onto a needle as a picked up stitch. This distorts the edge badly.

Instead, insert the crochet hook into the garment along the edge, catch the yarn from the ball, pull a loop through and slip that loop onto the knitting needle. This is a picked up stitch:

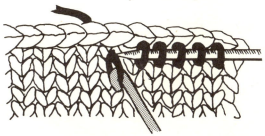

When working on a neckline or other edge, some stitches can be held on a needle holder. Do not simply transfer these to a needle, but knit them off and include them in the number of stitches to be picked up. The pick up row does not destroy a pattern stitch row, either— simply return to the pattern stitch on the next row.

Be a real eye-catcher with this double-button special...

Carousel Cardigan

A simple, no-problem pattern with two rows of buttons and comfortable raglan sleeves. One of the most popular styles for years.

Yarn: Knitting Worsted Weight 16 (20-20-24) oz.
Blocked Measurement: 36 (38-40-42) inches for sweater at bust.
Gauge: In stockinette stitch (ss) 4½ stitches (sts) per inch, 6 rows per inch.
Needles: Single point No. 6 and No. 9 or as needed to reach proper gauge.
Accessories: St holders.

BACK
Cast on 81 (87-91-95) sts using smaller needle. Rib as follows for 2 ins:
Row 1: P 1, k 1 across, end p 1 (right side).
Row 2: K 1, p 1 across, end k 1. End ready for right side row.
Change to larger needle and continue in pattern:
Row 1: P 1, *k 1 thru back loop (k 1 b), p 1, rep from * 3 times more, k 20 (23-25-27), p 1, **k 1 b, p 1, rep from ** 10 times more, k 20 (23-25-27), p 1, ***k 1 b, p 1, rep from *** 3 times more.
Row 2: P across.
Rep these two rows for pattern. When piece measures 13 ins from bottom of ribbing, start armhole. Check width: 18 (19-20-21) ins.

Armhole: Bind off 2 sts beg of next 2 rows. Work 2 (0-2-0) rows even. Dec for full-fashion armhole as follows:
Row 1: K 2, p 2 tog, work to last 4 sts, p 2 tog, k 2.
Row 2: P across row.
Rep these 2 rows until 23 sts remain. Place on holder.

RIGHT FRONT
Cast on 46 (48-52-54) sts using smaller needle. Rib in k 1, p 1 for 2 ins. Change to larger needles and continue as follows:
Row 1: (K 1 b, p 1) 12 sts, k 25 (27-31-33), p 1, *k 1 b, p 1 rep from * to end of row.
Row 2: P all sts.
Rep these 2 rows for pattern. When piece measures 13 ins from bottom of ribbing, start armholes. Check width: 10 (10½-11-11½) ins.

Armholes: Bind off 2 sts at armhole edge, p to end of row. Work next 2 rows even. Then dec for full-fashion armhole as on back for 27 (29-32-33) sts. *At the SAME TIME,* when armhole measures 6¼ (6¾-7¼-7¾) ins above underarm, work 10 (10-11-12) sts at front edge and place on a holder. Dec 1 st at same edge every other row 5 times. Continue armhole dec until 2 sts remain. Bind off.

LEFT FRONT
Same as right front, but reverse all shaping and pattern placement. Rib in (p 1, k 1). Fashion raglan dec same as on back.

SLEEVES (Make 2)
Cast on 36 (38-40-42) sts using smaller needles. Rib in k 1, p 1 for 2 ins, inc 4 sts evenly across last row. Change to larger needles and work in ss to 1¼ ins from top of ribbing. Inc 1 st each end of needle. Continue in ss for another 1¼ ins and inc 1 st each end of needle again. P next row. Next row p 1, k to last st, p 1. Rep the last 2 rows to 3¾ ins above ribbing. Inc 1 st each end of needle. P next row. Next row, k 1 b, p 1, k to last 2 sts, p 1, k 1 b. P next row. Continue this way to inc 1 st each end of needle every 1¼ ins 7 times more and to work added sts in pattern st for 60 (62-64-66) sts. When sleeve measures 17 (17½-18-18) ins from bottom of ribbing, start armhole.

Armhole:
Sizes 36 (38): Bind off 2 sts beg of next 2 rows. Work 2 (4) rows even. Make full-fashion dec as on back until 2 sts remain. Bind off.
Sizes 40 (42): Bind off 2 sts beg of next 2 rows. Make full-fashion dec every 4th row 4 times, then every other row until 2 sts remain. Bind off.

FINISHING
Set in sleeves.

Neck: With right side facing you and using smaller needles, pick up approximately 75 (77-79-81) sts around neck, including those on holders. Rib in k 1, p 1 for 2 ins, keeping 12 sts at each front edge in pattern rib as on fronts. Bind off *loosely in ribbing.* Sew side and sleeve seams. Turn neck ribbing in half to inside and tack down. Block to size. Sew grosgrain ribbon to back of front borders. Make machine buttonholes. Sew on buttons.

Look extra pretty in this feminine top, day and night...

Lacey Blouson

A pullover sweater so delicate looking you'll swear nature made it. For advanced knitters, this sweater should be worn loosely, for a softer shape.

Yarn: Fingering Weight 10 (10-12-12) oz.
Blocked Measurement: 38 (40-42-44) inches for sweater at bust.
Gauge: In stockinette stitch (ss) 7 stitches (sts) per inch.
Needles: Single point No. 4 or as needed to reach proper gauge.
Accessories: No. 1 steel crochet hook.

Lace Pattern: Multiple of 6 plus 1. Learn the pattern thoroughly so that when you get to the front neck dec you will be able to maintain the lace pattern. But if you should have trouble, it is quite satisfactory to simply work the balance of the front in ss. All other dec areas in the pattern have been carefully arranged so you will be at the proper place in the lace pattern.

Row 1: (Wrong side and all wrong side rows) P across row.
Row 2: K 1, *yo sl 1, k 1, psso (SKP), k 1, k 2 tog, yo, k 1, rep from * across row.
Row 4: K 1, *yo, k 1, sl 1, k 2 tog, psso, k 1, yo, k 1, rep from * across row.
Row 6: K 1, *k 2 tog, yo, k 1, yo, SKP, k 1, rep from * across row.
Row 8: K 2 tog, *(k 1, yo) twice, k 1, sl 1, k 2 tog, psso, rep from * to last 5 sts, then (k 1, yo) twice, k 1, SKP.

Rep these 8 rows for the pattern.

BACK

Cast on 103 (109-115-121) sts. Work in pattern st for 4 ins. Change to ss, starting on front side with k row. Work 4 rows in ss. Next row: K 3, *yo, k 2 tog, k 3, rep from * across row. Next 4 rows in ss. Start lace pattern again at row 1 and continue until piece measures 9 ins from beading row.

Armhole: Bind off 18 sts beg of next two rows. Continue in lace pattern as before until armhole measures 7½ (8-8½-9) ins from bind-off.

Shoulder: Bind off 6 sts beg next 4 rows and 0 (0-3-6) sts beg next 2 rows. Bind off balance: 43 (49-49-49) sts.

FRONT

Same as back to 5½ (6-6½-7) ins above armhole bind-off. Bind off center 19 (25-25-25) sts. Attach a second ball of yarn so you can work both sides of the neck at same time. Then bind off 6 sts at each neck edge 2 times. When armhole measures same as on back, bind off at each shoulder 6 sts twice and 0 (0-3-6) sts once. (See lace pattern notes).

SLEEVES (Make 2)

Cast on 85 (91-91-97) sts. Work in lace pattern st to 18 (18-18½-18½) ins (or desired length) from cast-on sts. Mark this point and work 3 ins more. Bind off all sts.

FINISHING

Sew side seams. Sew sleeve seam to the mark. Sew shoulder seams. Attach the 3 ins of the top of the sleeve seam to the long underarm bind-off, and sew the balance of the top of the sleeve into the armhole.

Bottom of Sweater: With No. 1 steel crochet hook, work shell st edge this way: Attach yarn, sc in next st, ch 1, *sk 2 sts (dc, ch 1) 3 times in next st, sk 2 sts, sc in next st, ch 1. Rep from * around bottom. Attach to the beg of the round and fasten off.

Neck: Attach yarn, ch 3, dc in same st, *ch 1, sk next st, dc in next st, ch 1, sk 1 st, 2 dc in next st, rep from * around neck. Next row: Work shell st as on bottom.

Sleeves: Same as bottom. Or if you wish to have a drawstring type of sleeve, then finish the sleeve with the same edge as the neck and make the same sort of cord.

Blocking: Block by stretching and flattening lace to the proper measurements. Make cord for neck and body. This can be crocheted or twisted rope, or even a velvet ribbon—whatever you desire.

A sweater so gorgeous you'll look for excuses to wear it...

Tall Trees

Picture-perfect leafy fronds decorate the back, front and sleeve ends of this beautiful sweater for a look you'll be noticed for. An involved knitting pattern with careful counting and watching required, this one is best for expert knitters.

Yarn: Sportsweight 12 (14-14) oz.
Blocked Measurement: 36 (38-40) inches for sweater at bust.
Gauge: In stockinette stitch (ss) 6 stitches (sts) per inch, 8 rows per inch.
Needles: Single point No. 3 and No. 5 or as needed to reach proper gauge.
Accessories: St holders.

BACK

Cast on 116 (122-130) sts with smaller needle. Rib in k 1, p 1 for 2 ins, inc one st at end of last row. Change to larger needles and continue:

Row 1: K 42 (45-49), place a marker on needle, p 13, p 2 tog, inc 1 st in next st, k 1, inc 1 st in next st, p 2 tog, p 13, place a marker on needle, k 42 (45-49).

Row 2: P 42 (45-49), sl marker, k 14, p 1, k 1, p 1, k 1, p 1, k 14, sl marker, p 42 (45-49).

Row 3: K 42 (45-49), p 12, p 2 tog, yo, p 1, yo, p 1, k 1, p 1, yo, p 1, yo, p 2 tog, p 12, k 42 (45-49).

Row 4: P 42 (45-49), k 13, p 3, inc 1 st in next st, p 1, inc 1 st in next st, p 3, k 13, p 42 (45-49).

Row 5: K 42 (45-49), p 11, p 2 tog, k 1, yo, k 1, yo, k 1, p 2, k 1, p 2, k 1, yo, k 1, yo, k 1, p 2 tog, p 11, k 42 (45-49).

Keeping beg and ending sts in ss, the balance of the pattern instructions will refer only to the 33 sts of the leaf pattern between the markers.

Row 6: K 12, p 5, k 1, inc 1 st in next st, p 1, inc 1 st in next st, k 1, p 5, k 12.

Row 7: P 10, p 2 tog, k 2, yo, k 1, yo, k 2, p 3, k 1, p 3, k 2, yo, k 1, yo, k 2, p 2 tog, p 10.

Row 8: K 11, p 7, k 1, inc 1 st in next st, k 1, p 1, k 1, inc 1 st in next st, k 1, p 7, k 11.

Row 9: P 9, p 2 tog, k 3, yo, k 1, yo, k 3, p 3, k 3, p 3, k 3, yo, k 1, yo, k 3, p 2 tog, p 9.

Row 10: K 10, p 9, k 1, inc 1 st in next st, k 1, p 3, k 1, inc 1 st in next st, k 1, p 9, k 10.

Row 11: P 8, p 2 tog, k 4, yo, k 1, yo, k 4, p 4, k 3, p 4, k 4, yo, k 1, yo, k 4, p 2 tog, p 8.

Row 12: K 9, p 11, k 1, inc 1 st in next st, k 2, p 3, k 2, inc 1 st in next st, k 1, p 11, k 9.

Row 13: P 7, p 2 tog, k 2 tog, k 7, k 2 tog, p 5, k 3, p 5, k 2 tog, k 7, k 2 tog, p 2 tog, p 7.

Row 14: K 8, p 9, k 5, inc 1 st in next st, p 1, inc 1 st in next st, k 5, p 9, k 8.

Row 15: P 6, p 2 tog, k 2 tog, k 5, k 2 tog, p 5, yo, p 1, yo, p 1, k 1, p 1, yo, p 1, yo, p 5, k 2 tog, k 5, k 2 tog, p 2 tog, p 6.

Row 16: K 7, p 7, k 5, p 3, inc 1 st in next st, p 1, inc 1 st in next st, p 3, k 5, p 7, k 7.

Row 17: P 5, p 2 tog, k 2 tog, k 3, k 2 tog, p 5, k 1, yo, k 1, yo, k 1, p 2, k 1, p 2, k 1, yo, k 1, yo, k 1, p 5, k 2 tog, k 3, k 2 tog, p 2 tog, p 5.

Row 18: K 6, p 5, k 5, p 5, k 1, inc 1 st in next st, p 1, inc 1 st in next st, k 1, p 5, k 5, p 5, k 6.

Row 19: P 4, p 2 tog, k 2 tog, k 1, k 2 tog, p 5, k 2, yo, k 1, yo, k 2, p 3, k 1, p 3, k 2, yo, k 1, yo, k 2, p 5, k 2 tog, k 1, k 2 tog, p 2 tog, p 4.

Row 20: K 5, p 3, k 5, p 7, k 1, inc 1 st in next st, k 1, p 1, k 1, inc 1 st in next st, k 1, p 7, k 5, p 3, k 5.

Row 21: P 3, p 2 tog, k 3 tog, p 5, k 3, yo, k 1, yo, k 3, p 3, k 3, p 3, k 3, yo, k 1, yo, k 3, p 5, k 3 tog, p 2 tog, p 3.

Continue to work sweater, rep rows 10-21 as often as desired. When piece measures 13 ins from the bottom, start armhole. Check width: 18 (19-20) ins.

Armholes: Bind off 2 (2-3) sts beg of next 2 rows. Work 2 (0-0) rows even. Dec 1 st at each end of needle every other row until 32 (32-34) sts remain. *AT THE SAME TIME* at about 1 in above the underarm or as soon thereafter as you complete row 21 of pattern, work your final pattern this way: Rep rows 10, 11, 12 as before. Then as follows:

Row 13a: K 1, p 6, p 2 tog, k 2 tog, k 7, k 2 tog,

CONTINUED ON NEXT PAGE

CONTINUED FROM PREVIOUS PAGE

p 6, yo, k 1, yo, p 6, k 2 tog, k 7, k 2 tog, p 2 tog, p 6, k 1.

Row 14a: P 1, k 7, p 9, k 6, p 3, k 6, p 9, k 7, p 1.

Row 15a: K 2, p 6, k 2 tog, k 5, k 2 tog, p 6, k 1, yo, k 1, yo, k 1, p 6, k 2 tog, k 5, k 2 tog, p 6, k 2.

Row 16a: P 2, k 6, p 7, k 6, p 5, k 6, p 7, k 6, p 2.

Row 17a: K 3, p 5, k 2 tog, k 3, k 2 tog, p 6, k 2, yo, k 1, yo, k 2, p 6, k 2 tog, k 3, k 2 tog, p 5, k 3.

Row 18a: P 3, k 5, p 5, k 6, p 7, k 6, p 5, k 5, p 3.

Row 19a: K 4, p 4, k 2 tog, k 1, k 2 tog, p 6, k 3, yo, k 1, yo, k 3, p 6, k 2 tog, k 1, k 2 tog, p 4, k 4.

Row 20a: P 4, k 4, p 3, k 6, p 9, k 6, p 3, k 4, p 4.

Row 21a: K 5, p 3, k 3 tog, p 6, k 4, yo, k 1, yo, k 4, p 6, k 3 tog, p 3 k 5.

Row 22a: P 5, k 10, p 11, k 10, p 5.

Row 23a: K 6, p 9, k 2 tog, k 7, k 2 tog, p 9, k 6.

Row 24a: P 6, k 9, p 9, k 9, p 6.

Row 25a: K 7, p 8, k 2 tog, k 5, k 2 tog, p 8, k 7.

Row 26a: P 7, k 8, p 7, k 8, p 7.

Row 27a: K 8, p 7, k 2 tog, k 3, k 2 tog, p 7, k 8.

Row 28a: P 8, k 7, p 5, k 7, p 8.

Row 29a: K 9, p 6, k 2 tog, k 1, k 2 tog, p 6, k 9.

Row 30a: P 9, k 6, p 3, k 6, p 9.

Row 31a: K 10, p 6, k 1, p 6, k 10.

Row 32a: P 10, k 6, p 1, k 6, p 10.

Row 33a: K 11, p 11, k 11.

Row 34a: P 11, k 11, p 11.

Row 35a: K 12, p 9, k 12.

Continue this way to change 1 more st at each side until there are 3 p sts left. At this point all sts are worked in ss. Continue to dec 1 st each end of needle every other row until 29 (29-31) sts are left at back of neck. Put on holder.

RIGHT FRONT

Cast on 64 (66-70) sts with smaller needle.

Row 1:   K 8, rib in (p 1, k 1) for balance of sts.

Row 2:   Rib in (p 1, k 1) to last 8 sts, p 8.

Rep the 2 rows for 2 ins. Change to larger needles and continue in pattern this way: K 8, p 1, k 7, place ring marker on needle, work pattern st as on back for next 33 sts, place a ring marker on needle, k 16 (18-22). Keep pattern as established, continue working until piece is the same length as back to armhole. Check width: 10 (10½-11) ins.

Armhole: Bind off 2 sts at armhole edge, work 4 (4-2) rows even. Dec 1 st at same edge every other row, as for the back. At the same time complete pattern at the same point as on the back. When piece measures 6½ (6¾-7½) ins above underarm, start neck.

Neckline: At center edge work 16 (16-17) sts and place them on holder. Dec 1 st at same edge every other row 5 times. Continue raglan to 2 sts. Bind off.

LEFT FRONT

Cast on 64 (66-70) sts with smaller needle.

Row 1: (K 1, p 1) to last 8 sts, k 8.

Row 2: P 8, (p 1, k 1) for balance of sts.

Continue as for right front reversing all shaping.

SLEEVES (Make 2)

Cast on 50 (52-54) sts on smaller needle. Rib in k 1, p 1 for 1 in. Change needles and inc 7 (7-9) sts evenly across row. Continue with pattern this way: Row 1: K 12 (13-14), place marker, work row 1 of pattern over next 33 sts, place marker, k 12 (13-14).

Continue with pattern st inc 1 st each end of needle every 1 in until there are 85 (89-93) sts on needle. *However,* when you have completed the first 21 rows of the pattern, continue as you would for a final rep. The balance of the sleeve will be in plain ss. When sleeve measures 15 ins, start underarm.

Armhole: Bind off 2 sts, beg of next 2 rows. Work 4 rows even. Dec 1 st each end of needle every other row until 3 sts remain. Bind off.

Sew in sleeves.

Neck: With right side facing and smaller needles, pick up approximately 109 (109-111) sts around neck. Rib in p 1, k 1 for 2 ins, keeping first and last 7 sts in ss. Bind off loosely in ribbing.

FINISHING

Sew sleeve and side seams. Block to size. Face front edges with grosgrain and make machine buttonholes. Turn neck ribbing in half to the inside and tack in place.

The perfect mix-and-match separate for your wardrobe...

Woman's Pullover Vest

A terrific little vest, at left, with easy instructions for both crew and v-neck styles. It's good looking with skirts, slacks and all your prettiest blouses.

Yarn: Sportsweight 8 (8-10-12) oz.
Blocked Measurement: 34 (36-38-40) inches for vest at bust.
Gauge: In stockinette stitch (ss) 5½ stitches (sts) per inch.
Needles: Single point No. 3, No. 6, or as needed to reach proper gauge. Double point No. 4.
Accessories: 2 st holders.

BACK

Cast on 94 (100-104-110) sts using smaller needles. Rib in k 1, p 1 for 2 ins. Change to larger needles. Continue in ss straight to 13 ins from bottom of ribbing. Blocked width of piece: 17 (18-19-20) ins.

Armhole: Bind off 6 sts beg of next 2 rows. Dec 1 st every other row at each armhole edge 10 (12-13-14) times. Continue straight to 8 (8¼-8½-8¾) ins from underarm.

Shoulder: Bind off 6 sts beg of next 4 rows, and 6 (6-7-8) sts beg of next 2 rows. Place remaining 26 (28-28-30) sts on a holder.

FRONT

Crew Neck: Same as back to 5½ (5¾-6-6¼) ins above underarm bind-off. Place center 14 (16-16-18) sts on a holder. Attach a 2nd ball of yarn so you can work both sides of neck at the same time. Dec 1 st at each neck edge every other row 6 times. When armhole measures same as on back, bind off at each shoulder edge 6 sts 2 times and 6 (6-7-8) sts 1 time.

V-Neck: Same as back to underarm. Divide sts evenly, attaching a 2nd ball of yarn so you can work both sides of neck opening on each row. Working armhole edge same as on back, dec 1 st at each neck edge every 4th row 13 (14-14-15) times. When armhole is same length as on back, bind off at each shoulder edge 6 sts 2 times and 6 (6-7-8) sts 1 time.

FINISHING

Sew shoulder seams.

Crew Neck: With right side facing you and using dp needles, pick up approximately 78 (80-80-86) sts around neck. Rib in k 1, p 1, for 2 ins. Bind off *loosely in ribbing.* Fold ribbing in half to inside and tack down.

V-Neck: With right side facing you and using dp needles, pick up 26 (28-28-30) sts across back of neck and 49 (51-53-55) sts on each front. Place a marker ring on needle at "V." Rib in k 1, p 1 to 2 sts before marker, k 2 tog, sl marker, sl 1, k 1, psso. Complete round in ribbing rep dec sts on each side of marker each row for 1 in. Then continue rib, inc 1 st each side of marker each row for 1 in. Bind off *loosely in ribbing.* Fold ribbing in half to inside of neck and tack down.

Both styles: Sew side seams.

Armhole bands: With right side facing you, and using dp needles, pick up 88 (90-92-94) sts around armhole. Rib in k 1, p 1 for 2 ins. Bind off *loosely in ribbing.* Turn half of ribbing to inside and tack down.

Be A Knit Whiz...

Count to be sure

When you find yourself in trouble with a pattern stitch, the *first* thing to do is always recount the number of stitches. Often, people have problems because they have the wrong number of stitches, even though they swear they have them right.

Calling all mothers and daughters...

Fiesta Skirt

The sharpest skirt this side of the border! When there's a mother-daughter fling coming up, why not try this cute little skirt... in both children's and adult's sizes. (See our choice of hot colors on page 86 with the child's pattern). Easy circular knitting, and lots of fun to do!

Yarn: Knitting Worsted Weight, 2 skeins color A, 1 skein color B, and 1 skein color C.
Size: S-M-L
Gauge: In stockinette stitch (ss) 4 stitches (sts) per inch.
Needles: No. 10 circular needle or as needed to reach proper gauge.

SKIRT
With color A cast on 142 (148-156) sts. Join, being careful not to twist sts. Work in k 1, p 1 ribbing for 4 rows. Then *k 1, k 2 tog, yo; rep from * around. Change to color B and work 4 rows in k 1, p 1 rib. Inc 26 sts evenly around needle.

**Change to color C and continue in all k st. Work color C for 1 in, then 1 round color A, 2 rounds color C, 1 round color A, 2 ins color B.

3 rounds color A, 2 rounds color B, 1 round color A, 1 round color C.

1 round color A, 1 in color C, 1 round color A, 1 round color C, 1 round color B.

1 in color A, 3 rounds color B, 1 round color C.

2 ins color A, 3 rounds color C, 2 rounds color B.

1 round color A, 1 round color C, 1 round color A, 1 in color B.

1 round color A, 1 round color B, 1 round color C.

3 rounds color B, 1 in color A, 1 round color B, 1 round color A, 1 round color B, 2 ins color A.

3 rounds color C, 1 round color B, 3 rounds color C, 1 round color A, 1 round color B. To lengthen skirt rep from ** to desired length. Then go directly to "bottom."

Bottom: With color A, *k 1, k 2 tog, yo, rep from * around row. Work 2 rows k 1, p 1. Bind off loosely.

FINISHING
Make a crochet cord. Ch desired length and work 1 sc in each ch. Thread through holes in waistband. Attach tassels and wooden beads.

Be A Knit Whiz...

Changing colors of yarn

When you change colors in knitting, always be sure to cross the strands of yarn so there

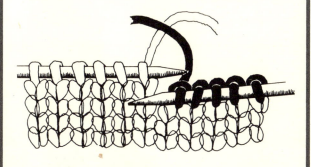

won't be a hole in your knitting.
   Leave a 3-inch end of the new color yarn to weave into garment's wrong side when finished. Carry colors loosely across the wrong side.

Relax—it's comfortable and care-free for the life you lead...

The Northerner

The look and feel of real comfort is what this bulky cowl neck pullover gives. Three-quarter length sleeves can be turned up or worn down for an easy, uncomplicated look. And what a stylish look it is!

Yarn: Bulky 28 (30-32) oz.
Blocked Measurement: 36 (38-40-42) inches for sweater at bust.
Gauge: In stockinette stitch (ss) 3½ stitches (sts) per inch.
Needles: Straight No. 9 and No. 10½ or as needed to reach required gauge.
Accessories: Ring Markers.

Pattern Stitch: Mock English Rib (multiple of 4, plus 3) *k 2, p 2; repeat from * across row ending k 2, p 1. Repeat this pattern on both sides of knitting.

BACK OF PULLOVER
Cast on 63 (67-71-75) sts using smaller needles. Work in pattern for 2½ ins. Change to larger needles & continue in pattern st straight to 14 ins from bottom of piece. Blocked measurement of piece: 18 (19-20-21) ins.

Armhole: Bind off 10 sts beg of next 2 rows. Continue straight to 8½ (9-9½-9¾) ins from bind off row.

Shoulder: Bind off 5 sts beg of next 2 rows; and 5 (6-7-8) sts beg of next 2 rows. Bind off balance of 23 (25-27-29) sts.

FRONT OF PULLOVER
Same as back to 5 (5½-6-6¼) ins above underarm. Start neck: bind off 13 (15-17-19) center sts. Using separate balls of yarn on each side of neck, bind off 2 sts at each neck edge every other row 2 times and 1 st 1 time. Continue straight until armhole measures same as on back. Bind off at each shoulder edge 5 sts 1 time and 5 (6-7-8) sts 1 time.

SLEEVES (Make 2)
Cast on 51 (55-59-59) sts using larger needle. Work in pattern st straight to 16 (16¼-16½-16¾) oms or as desired. Place a marker on knitting at this point to mark armhole. Continue straight in pattern st for 3 more ins. Bind off all sts.

FINISHING
Sew shoulder seams and side seams. Sew sleeve seams up to markers.

Inserting sleeves: Place the 3 ins of un-sewn portion of sleeve seam on each side of side seam at armhole to form base. Sew balance of sleeve cap into armhole.

Collar: Cast on 95 (99-103-103) sts using smaller needles. Work in pattern for 2½ ins. Change to larger needles & continue in pattern until piece measures 7½ ins. Bind off *loosely* in pattern. Sew ends of collar to form circle. Attach to neck placing seam at back of neck, sewing on cast-on edge.

Knit-Picking...

"Don'ts" for knitters

1. Don't measure loosely. Make sure the person being measured is standing erect.
2. Don't measure an old sweater. It has usually been stretched through wear.
3. Don't guess. You'll usually guess a women's size too small and a man's too large.
4. Don't measure over coats or jackets—unless the sweater will be worn that way.
5. Don't knit in a vacuum. If something looks wrong, hot-foot it to your yarn shop.

31

Just right…for a special couple you know…

String Shirt

If you like comfort and style in casual knits, our his and her shirts are sure to fit the bill. (Men's shirt pattern page 64.) Adjustable sleeves and no wrong side—the same K 2, P 2 ribs inside and out!

Yarn: Sportsweight 14 (16-16) oz.
Blocked Measurement: 36 (38-40-42) inches for shirt at bust.
Gauge: In stockinette stitch (ss) 6 stitches (sts) per inch.
Needles: Single point No. 4 and No. 5.
Accessories: Crochet Hook No. 0 steel. 3 st holders.

BACK
Cast on 108 (114-120-126) sts using No. 4 needle. Work in ss for 1¼ ins. K 1 row on the p side. Change to No. 5 needles and continue in ss straight to 14 ins from the hem row. Blocked width of piece: 18 (19-20-21) ins.

Armhole: Bind off 2 (2-2-3) sts beg of next 2 rows. On the next row change from ss to a k 2, p 2 rib st. Dec 1 st each end of the needle every other row until 28 (30-32-34) sts remain. Place them on a holder.

FRONT
Work the same as the back to 1 in above the underarm. On the next row bind off the center 2 sts. Add a second ball of yarn and work both sides at the same time. Continue with the raglan dec until 14 (15-16-17) sts remain on each side of the center opening. Put them on a holder.

SLEEVES (Make 2)
Cast on 82 (86-90-94) sts with No. 5 needle. Work in k 2, p 2 ribbing, straight to 12 ins from the start.

Armhole: Bind off 2 (2-2-3) sts beg of the next 2 rows. Dec 1 st at each end of the needle every other row until 2 sts remain. Bind off.

Sew sleeve seams into the body.

Collar: With the *inside* facing you and No. 4 needle, pick up 60 (64-68-72) sts around the neck including the sts on the holders. Follow the established k 2 p 2 pattern and adjust the number of sts if necessary, so the ribbing sequence is not disrupted. Work for 3½ ins. Bind off loosely in ribbing. Sew side and sleeve seams. Work 2 rows of sc on each side of the front of opening. Lap these rows at the bottom and tack in place. Turn up hem at the bottom.

This shirt looks best when ironed quite flat. Use a cool steam iron and proceed with caution. The shirt is designed to be a loose garment. Choose a size which will give you sufficient room.

A fashion classic just right for any season...

Swagger Jacket

This bulky woman's jacket is a twin to our men's swagger jacket (see page 60), and because it's worked on big needles, it's big on comfort too. The shawl collar is made separately and sewed on. Big pockets and a tie belt pull it all together.

Yarn: Bulky 17 (19) 2 oz balls or Knitting Worsted Weight 8 (9) 4 oz balls.
Blocked Measurement: 38 (42) inches for sweater at chest.
Gauge: In stockinette stitch (ss) 3½ stitches (sts) per inch; 5 rows per inch.
Needles: No. 10 and No. 10½ or as needed to reach proper gauge. 29 inch No. 10 circular needle.

BACK
Cast on 66 (72) sts with smaller needles. Rib in k 2, p 2 for 1½ ins. Change needles. Continue in ss straight to 17 ins from bottom.

Armhole: Bind off 2 sts beg of next 2 rows. Work 2 (4) rows even. Dec 1 st each end of needle every other row this way: K 2, p 2 tog k to last 4 sts, p tog, k 2. P the next row. Rep last 2 rows until 16 (18) sts remain. Bind off.

RIGHT FRONT
Cast on 34 (38) sts with smaller needle. Rib in k 2, p 2 for 1½ ins. Change to larger needles and continue in ss to 17 ins from bottom. Mark one edge for armhole and one for neck.

Armhole: Bind off 2 sts at armhole edge and dec 1 st at neck edge. Work 2 (4) rows even. Dec 1 st at armhole edge every other row in the same fashion as for the back. Rep neck dec every 4th row 7 (9) times more. Continue raglan to 2 sts. Bind off.

LEFT FRONT
Same as right front but reverse shaping.

SLEEVES (Make 2)
Cast on 38 (42) sts on circular needle. Rib in k 2, p 2 for 1½ ins. Change needles and work in ss. Inc 1 st each end of needle every 2 ins until 50 (54) sts. Continue straight to 17 ins from bottom.

Armhole: Bind off 2 sts beg of next 2 rows. Work 4 rows even. Dec 1 st each end of needle every other row in same fashion as for the back. When 2 sts remain, bind off.

Sew in sleeves. Sew body and sleeve seams.

COLLAR
Cast on 226 (230) sts on smaller needle. Work in k 2, p 2 for 8 rows. Bind off 56 sts beg of next 2 rows, 2 sts beg of next 10 (12) rows, 7 sts beg of next 6 rows, 8 sts beg of next 4 rows. Bind off balance 20 sts.

POCKETS (Make 2)
Cast on 26 sts with smaller needle. Rib in k 2, p 2, for 7 inches. Bind off.

BELT
Cast on 14 sts using smaller needle. *K 1, yarn forward, sl 1 as to p; rep from * across row. Work all rows alike. Make belt 50 ins long or as desired.

FINISHING
Assemble jacket.

Attach collar to jacket, using the bound-off edge of the collar as the seam edge, as follows: (1) Tack center point of bound-off edge of collar to center point of back of neck; (2) tack ends of collar piece to the respective front edges at the bottom of the jacket; (3) the points where the collar starts inc in width should be tacked to the points where the front edges of the jacket start the V-neck dec. Complete sewing collar to jacket, easing the seam around the front edges and neckline so it will lay smoothly.

Place pockets at bottom of fronts in positions most comfortable to you.

Make belt loops by sc leftover yarn.

Add a little pizzazz to your wardrobe when you're on the go...

The Runabout Tunic

An up-to-the-minute look that's tops in comfort and tops in style. Loose, three-quarter length raglan sleeves, a square neck and simple construction make this tunic something perfect to wear right now.

Yarn: Sportsweight 12 (14-14) oz.
Blocked Measurement: 36 (38-40) inches for sweater at bust.

Gauge: In stockinette stitch (ss) 5½ stitches (sts) per inch, 7½ rows per inch.

Needles: No. 5 for hem, No. 6 for body, and No. 4 for ribbing or as needed to reach proper gauge.

BACK

Cast on 107 (113-117) sts using No. 5 needle. Work in ss for 10 rows. K one row on wrong side (hem row). Change to No. 6 needle. Continue in ss, starting with a k row. When 3 ins from hem row, dec 1 st each end of next k row. Continue in ss dec 1 st at each end of needle every 2 ins 3 times more. You should have 99 (105-109) sts on needle; piece should measure 18 (19-20) ins wide in blocked position. Continue straight to 13 ins from hem row.

Armhole (Raglan Shaping): Bind off 5 sts beg of next 2 rows.

Dec row 1: K 2, sl 1, k 1, psso, K to last 4 sts, k 2 tog, k 2. P next row. Rep dec row 1, 21 (23-24) times more till 45 (47-49) sts are left on needle.

Dec row 2: Change to No. 4 needle. K 2, sl 1, k 1, psso, p 1 k 1 in ribbing to last 4 sts, k 2 tog, k 2. Continue in ribbing pattern, dec as in dec row 2, every other row 5 times more until 33 (35-37) sts left. Bind off *loosely* in ribbing.

FRONT

Same as back.

SLEEVES (Make 2)

Cast on 81 (85-87) sts using No. 5 needle. Work in ss for 10 rows. K one row on wrong side (hem row). Starting with next row as a k row, work in ss for 11 ins from hem row.

Armhole (Raglan shaping): Work raglan shaping as on back with *dec row 1* until 27 (29-29) sts are left. Work *dec row 2* until 15 (17-17) sts remain. Bind off *loosely* in ribbing.

FINISHING

Sew sleeves into body. Sew side and sleeve seams. Turn up hems on body and sleeves and tack in place.

Light, fresh and as simple as a charm to make...

Glitter Shell

This dainty dress-up shell (next page) is perfect for fancy, sparkling yarns. The pattern lets fancy yarns predominate, and delicately scalloped edges make it elegant to wear.

Yarn: Fingering Weight 6 (6-7-7) oz.
Blocked Measurement: 34 (36-38-40) inches for shell at bust.
Gauge: In stockinette stitch (ss) 7 stitches (sts) per inch.
Needles: Single point No. 3 or as needed to reach proper gauge.
Accessories: No. 1 steel crochet hook.

BACK

Cast on 106 (114-122-128) sts. Work in ss inc 1 st at each end of needle every 1½ ins, 6 times—118 (126-134-140) sts. Work straight to 13½ ins from the bottom. Blocked width: 17 (18-19-20) ins.

Armhole: Bind off 10 sts beg of next 2 rows. Dec 1 st every other row, st each armhole edge 12 (12-13-13) times. Work straight until armhole measures 6 (6¼-6¾-7) ins above the armhole bind-off.

Neck and shoulders: Bind off center 32 (38-42-46) sts. Attach a 2nd ball of yarn so you can work both sides at the same time. Bind off 2 sts at each neck edge 2 times. When the armhole measures 7 (7¼-7¾-8) ins, bind off at each shoulder, 9 sts once and 8 (9-10-11) sts once.

FRONT

Same as back to 2½ (2½-3-3¼) ins from the underarm. Bind off center 22 (28-32-36) sts. Attach a 2nd ball of yarn so you can work both sides of the neck at the same time. Bind off 2 sts at each neck edge 3 times and then dec 1 st at each neck edge every other row 3 times. When armhole measures the same as back, bind off at each shoulder 9 sts once and 8 (9-10-11) sts once.

CONTINUED ON NEXT PAGE

An accent for your hair and shoulders that's oh so delicate and pretty...

Luster Lace Head Scarf

The fancy pattern stitches on the rectangular evening scarf we've shown at right aren't for beginners, because it gets difficult to see what you're doing on such big needles. But wow—what a look!

Yarn: Any fine, metallic yarn, 7 oz.
Needles: No. 10½.

Pattern Stitch (63 sts):
Row 1:   (K 1, p 1) twice, *skp, k 3b, yo, k 1, yo, k 3b, k 2 tog, rep from * to last 4 sts, (k 1, p 1) twice.
Row 2:   And all even number rows: (P 1, k 1) twice, p to last 4 sts, (p 1, k 1) twice.
Row 3:   (K 1, p 1) twice, skp, k 2b, yo, k 1, yo, skp, yo, k 2b, k 2 tog; rep from * to last 4 sts, (k 1, p 1) twice.
Row 5:   (K 1, p 1) twice, *skp, k 1b, yo, k 1, yo, (skp, yo) twice, k 1b, k 2 tog; rep from * to last 4 sts, (k 1, p 1) twice.
Row 7:   (K 1, p 1) twice, *skp, yo, k 1, (yo, skp) 3 times, yo, k 2 tog; rep from * to last 4 sts, (k 1, p 1) twice.
Row 8:   Same as row 2.

SCARF

Cast on 63 sts. Work above pattern 2 times (16 rows); then work 8 rows of garter st.
Row 25:   *K 1 st wrapping yarn 3 times around needle; rep across row.
Row 26:   K each st dropping the additional wraps to make a long st.
Rows 27 to 34: Work these 8 rows in garter st.

Rep the above 34 rows as often as you like until you reach the length of scarf you want. End the scarf with 2 lace patterns (rows 1-16).

Block out flat so that you have a thin, lacy scarf.

CONTINUED FROM PREVIOUS PAGE
FINISHING
Sew shoulder and side seams. Block to desired size. Then work 1 row of sc on all edges—neck, armholes, and bottom. To make a nice finish, we added a shell border. Any shell pattern is suitable. The one we used is one of the simplest. At the end of the 1 row of sc, join the end, ch 2, work 2 dc in the first sc, *skip 2 sc, and work 1 sc in the next sc, sk 2 sc, and in the next sc work 1 sc, 3 dc, 1 sc—that's one shell. Rep from * around edge. Finish off.

k 1, psso, yo, sl 1—k2 tog—psso; rep from *: end last rep (sl 1, k 1, psso) instead of sl 1, k 2 tog-psso.

Row 8:   K 1, *(yo, sl 1, k 1, psso) twice, k 3, (k 2 tog, yo) twice, k 1; rep from *.

Row 10:   K 1, *k 1, (yo, sl 1, k 1, psso) twice, k 1, (k 2 tog, yo) twice, k 2, rep from *.

Row 12:   K 1, *k 2, yo, sl 1, k 1, psso, yo, sl 1—k 2 tog—psso, yo, k 2 tog, yo, k 3; rep from *.

Finishing: Fringe and block out so the pattern is visible.

Set off a starlight mood of romance...

Black Diamond Shawl

Enjoy the look of real elegance for nighttime glamour with the glittery stole at right. A delicate lacy pattern makes it dressy.

Yarn: Sportsweight, five 2-oz balls.
Needles: No. 10½.

Cast on 73 sts. Work in pattern st for 60 ins. Bind off loosely in pattern st. Cut balance of yarn into 6 in lengths and fringe each end.

Row 1:   (Wrong side and all odd numbered rows): P.

Row 2:   K 1, *k 1, (k 2 tog, yo) twice, k 1, (yo, sl 1, k 1, psso) twice, k 2; rep from *.

Row 4:   K 1, *(k 2 tog, yo) twice, k 3, (yo, sl 1, k 1, psso) twice, k 1; rep from *.

Row 6:   K 2 tog, *yo, k 2 tog, yo, k 5, yo, sl 1,

Take flight into a dream of romance...

Honey Bee Shawl

Drape this delicate shawl over exciting evening clothes or daytime wear too! Dainty "wings" done in a lacy stitch accent this versatile triangular beauty.

Yarn: Five, 40-gram balls of any light mohair yarn.

Approximate width of shawl: 70½ inches.

Gauge: In seed stitch, 4 stitches (sts) per inch.

Needles: A 29 inch, No. 10½ circular needle, or as needed to reach proper gauge in seed stitch. Or, start with No. 10½ single point needles, shifting to the circular needle when the shawl gets too large to handle on single point needles.

Note: If you are not accustomed to knitting a lacy stitch, practice patterns A and B below before starting the shawl. Use scraps of knitting worsted weight yarn. Cast on 24 sts and work patterns A and B for 12 rows. The number of sts in pattern B will vary with each row until row 6 when you will have 12 sts on the needle again in pattern B.

Pattern Stitches Used:

Seed Stitch:
*K 1, p 1, rep from *; all rows the same. *Remember: In seed st, work a k st over a p st, and a p st over a k st.*

Faggotting (Pattern A):
Row 1: P 1, k 2, yo, sl 1 k 1 psso, p 1.
Row 2: K 1, p 2, yo, p 2 tog, k 1.
Rep rows 1 and 2.

Honey Bee (Pattern B):
Row 1: K 4, k 2 tog, yo, sl 1 k 1 psso, k 4.
Row 2: P 3, p 2 tog thru back loops (p 2 tog-B), drop yo of prior row off needle, yo twice, p 2 tog, p 3.
Row 3: K 2, k 2 tog, drop yo's of prior row off needle, yo 3 times, sl 1, k 1, psso, k 2.
Row 4: P 1, p 2 tog-B, drop yo's of prior row off needle, yo 4 times, p 2 tog, p 1.
Row 5: K 2 tog, drop yo's of prior row off needle, cast on 4 sts on right hand needle, insert needle under 4 loose strands and pull up a loop, yo, insert needle as before and draw up another loop, cast on 4 sts on right hand needle, sl 1, k 1, psso.

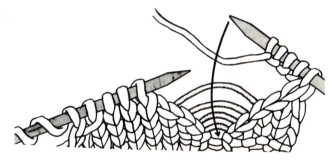

Insert needle under 4 loose strands...

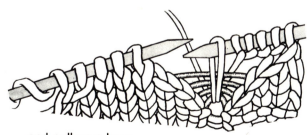

...and pull up a loop.

Row 6: P 5, p 2 tog (1 loop and following yo), p 6. Rep above 6 rows.

THE HONEY BEE SHAWL
Cast on 12 sts. Work in seed st. Inc 1 st each end of needle every row until shawl is completed. When
CONTINUED ON NEXT PAGE

will have 12 sts in that pattern once again.

Continue in seed st and patterns A and B for 23 more rows (sts on needle = 114).

Important: Be sure to inc in 1st and last sts each row as directed, working new sts into seed st pattern.

Next row: Inc 1 st in first st, work seed st over next 8 sts, place new marker on needle, work pattern A over next 6 sts, pattern B over next 12 sts, pattern A over next 6 sts, and pattern B over next 12 sts. Drop old marker, work patterns A, B and A, drop old marker, work in patterns B, A, B and A, place new marker on needle, work seed st for next 8 sts, inc 1 st in last st. Continue as before, inc 1 st each end of needle every row in seed st area, working seed st and patterns A and B in proper sequence for 35 more rows (sts on needle = 186).

Next row: Reset markers as before, this way: Inc 1 st in first st, work next 8 sts in seed st, place new marker, work alternating patterns as follows—A, B, A, B, drop old marker, A, B, A, B, A, B, A, B, A, B, A, drop old marker, B, A, B, A, set new marker, seed st for next 8 sts, inc 1 st in last st. Continue in pattern as established for 35 more rows (sts on needle = 258).

Next row: Reset markers as before by inc 1 st in first st, work next 8 sts in seed st, alternate patterns A and B until 9 sts remain, work 8 sts in seed st, inc 1 st in last st. Continue with established pattern until 282 sts on needle. *Continue without increasing,* working entire row in seed st for 4 more rows. Bind off in pattern.

Finishing: Cut remaining yarn into 12-in lengths. Fringe both slanted edges using 2 strands per knot, each knot being ½ to ¾ ins apart.

CONTINUED FROM PREVIOUS PAGE

there are 66 sts on needle start lace pattern this way: Inc 1 st in first st, work seed st over next 20 sts, place marker on needle. Work pattern A over next 6 sts, pattern B over next 12 sts and pattern A over next 6 sts. Place marker on needle, work seed st over next 20 sts, inc 1 st in last st.

Note: The number of sts in pattern B will vary on each row until the 6th row of that pattern when you

---

Knit-Picking...

Make it "terrific"

Garment manufacturers often care only to make an acceptable garment for the least possible cost. The hand knitter, however, can make the finest garment she is capable of knitting with the best yarn she can afford.

Any knitters who want to become accomplished should be prepared to knit, purl and rip—then knit, purl and rip again.

A well-made sweater will serve you for many years—don't waste all those shining hours by failing to read the hints in this book!

*Let him discover the joy of
classic comfort, wherever he goes...*

Cardigan Raglan Sleeve Sweater

Men's shoulders get cold too, and this pattern makes a garment just as versatile as our classic cardigan raglan shown on page 6 of the women's sweater section. Knit in crew or v-neck styles.

Yarn: Worsted Weight 20 (24-24) oz.
Blocked Measurement: 38 (42-46) inches for sweater at chest.
Gauge: In stockinette stitch (ss) 4½ stitches per inch, 6 rows per inch.
Needles: Single point No. 6 and No. 9 or as needed to reach proper gauge.
Accessories: 3 st holders.

BACK
Cast on 86 (94-104) sts with smaller needles. Rib in k 1, p 1 for 2½ ins. Change to larger needles and continue in ss straight to 16 ins from the bottom of the ribbing. Blocked measurement: 19 (21-23) ins across.

Armhole: Bind off 2 (2-3) sts beg of the next 2 rows. Work 4 (2-0) rows even. Dec 1 st every other row at each armhole edge until 24 (26-28) sts remain. For crew neck, place on holder. For v-neck, bind off.

RIGHT FRONT
Cast on 48 (52-56) sts with smaller needles. Rib in k 1, p 1 for 2½ ins. Keeping the center edge 8 sts in k 1, p 1 for the border, change to larger needles and continue in ss to 16 ins from the bottom.

Crew neck and armhole: Bind off 2 (2-3) sts at armhole edge. Work 4 (2-0) rows even. Dec 1 st at armhole edge every other row as for the back. At the same time when the sweater measures 7 (7½-8) ins above underarm, start neck.

Neckline: At center edge place 12 (13-13) sts on a holder. Dec 1 st at the same edge every other row 5 times. Continue raglan dec to 0 sts.

V-neck and armhole: Bind off 2 (2-3) sts at armhole edge. Work to last 10 sts, k 2 tog (neck dec), work border. Continue as established doing all neck dec just inside the 8 border sts. At armhole edge work 4 (2-0) rows even then dec raglan as on the back. Dec neck edge 1 st every 7 (6-7) rows 8 (9-9) times more. When only the 8 border sts remain, continue on them for another 2½ ins. Bind off.

LEFT FRONT
Same as the right front but *reverse shaping.* Rib in p 1, k 1.

SLEEVES (Make 2)
Cast on 44 (44-46) sts on smaller needles. Rib in k 1, p 1 for 2 ins. Change to larger needles and inc 6 sts evenly across row. Work in ss and inc 1 st each end of needle every 1¼ ins until 68 (70-76) sts. Continue straight to 17½ (18-18½) ins from the bottom.

Armhole: Bind off 2 sts beg of next 2 rows. Work 0 (2-0) rows even. Dec 1 st each end of needle every other row until 2 sts remain. Bind off.

Sew in sleeves. Sew side and sleeve seam.

Crew neck: With right side facing you and smaller needles, pick up 81 (83-85) sts around neck. Rib in k 1, p 1 for 1 in. Bind off *loosely* in ribbing.

V-neck: Sew the band tog and attach it to the back of the sweater neck.

Face each front edge with preshrunk grosgrain ribbon. Make machine buttonholes and sew on buttons.

Cardigan Set-in Sleeve Sweater

Make him a sweater he'll find a lot of uses for. And try a handsome tweed yarn or solid color that will fit his needs exactly. Again, available in crew and v-neck looks, this sweater is popular with all ages.

Yarn: Worsted Weight 20 (24-24) oz.
Blocked Measurement: 38 (42-46) inches for sweater at chest.
Gauge: In stockinette stitch (ss) 4½ stitches (sts) per inch.
Needles: Single point No. 6 and No. 9 or as needed to reach proper gauge.
Accessories: 3 st holders.

BACK

Cast on 86 (94-104) sts using smaller needles. Rib in k 1, p 1 for 2½ ins. Change to larger needles and continue in ss straight to 16 ins from the bottom of the ribbing. Blocked measurement: 19 (21-23) ins wide.

Armhole: Bind off 4 (5-5) sts beg of next 2 rows. Dec 1 st every other row at each armhole edge 4 (5-7) times. Continue straight to 9½ (10-10½) ins from bind-off.

Shoulder: Bind off 8 sts beg of next 4 rows, and 7 (8-10) sts beg of next 2 rows. For crew neck place balance 24 (26-28) sts on a holder. For v-neck, bind off.

RIGHT FRONT

Cast on 48 (52-56) sts using smaller needles. Rib in k 1, p 1 for 2½ ins. Keeping center edge 8 sts in k 1, p 1 for the border, change to larger needles and continue in ss to 16 ins from bottom of ribbing. Blocked measurement: 10½ (11½-12½) ins wide.

Crew neck and armhole: Bind off 4 (5-5) sts at armhole edge. Dec 1 st at the same edge every other row 4 (5-7) times. Continue straight to 7 (7½-8) ins. At the center edge, place 12 (13-13) sts on a holder. Dec 1 st at the same edge every other row 5

times. When armhole measures the same as back, bind off at each shoulder 8 sts 2 times and 7 (8-10) sts 1 time.

V-neck and armhole: Bind off 4 (4-5) sts at armhole edge. Work to last 10 sts, k 2 tog (neck dec), work border. Continue as established doing all neck dec just inside the 8 border sts. Dec at the armhole edge 1 st every other row 4 (5-7) times. At the same time dec at the neck edge 1 st every 7 (6-7) rows 8 (9-9) times more. When armhole measures the same as back, bind off at each shoulder 8 sts 2 times and 7 (8-10) sts 1 time. Continue on the 8 border sts for another 2½ ins. Bind off.

LEFT FRONT

Same as right front but *reverse shaping*. Rib in p 1, k 1.

SLEEVES (Make 2)

Cast on 44 (44-46) sts using smaller needles. Rib in k 1, p 1 for 2 ins. Change to larger needles and inc 6 sts evenly across row. Work in ss and inc 1 st each end of needle every 1 in until 68 (70-76) sts. Continue straight to 17½ (18-18½) ins from bottom.

Armhole: Bind off 4 (5-5) sts beg of next 2 rows. Dec 1 st each end of needle every other row for 5 (5½-6) ins. Bind off 2 sts beg of next 4 rows. Bind off balance.

FINISHING

Sew shoulder seams, sleeve seams, and side seams. Insert sleeves into armholes.

Crew neck: With right side facing you and using smaller needles, pick up 81 (83-85) sts around neck. Rib in k 1, p 1 for 1 in. Bind off *loosely* in ribbing.

V-neck: Sew neck band tog and attach it to the back neck of sweater. Face each front edge with preshrunk grosgrain ribbon. Make machine buttonholes and sew on buttons.

When what he likes is the natural, masculine look, knit a...

Pullover Raglan Sleeve Sweater

For some, this classic sweater would be a "back to basics" look. But for others, it's the simple, good taste in sweaters they've always loved. In crew and v-neck styles.

Yarn: Worsted Weight 20 (20-24) oz.
Blocked Measurement: 38 (42-46) inches for sweater at chest.
Gauge: In stockinette stitch (ss) 4½ stitches (sts) per inch, 6 rows per inch.
Needles: Single point No. 6 and No. 9 or as needed to reach proper gauge. Double point No. 6.
Accessories: 2 st holders.

BACK

Cast on 86 (94-104) sts using smaller needles. Work in k 1, p 1 for 2½ ins. Change to larger needles and continue in ss straight to 16 ins from the bottom. Blocked measurement: 19 (21-23) ins across.

Armhole: Bind off 2 (2-3) sts beg of next 2 rows. Work 2 (2-0) rows even. Dec 1 st every other row at each armhole edge until 24 (26-28) sts remain. Place on a holder.

FRONT

Crew neck: Same as back to 7 (7½-8) ins above underarm. Place center 14 (14-16) sts on a holder. Attach a 2nd ball of yarn so you can work both sides of neck at the same time. Dec 1 st at each neck edge every other row 5 (6-6) times. At the same time continue the raglan dec to 0 sts.

V-neck: Same as back to underarm. Divide sts evenly; attach a 2nd ball of yarn so you can work both sides of neck at the same time. Working the armhole the same as on the back, dec 1 st at each neck edge every 5 rows 12 (13-14) times. Continue the raglan to 0 sts.

SLEEVES (Make 2)

Cast on 44 (44-46) sts with smaller needles. Rib in k 1, p 1 for 2½ ins. Change to larger needles and inc 6 sts evenly across row. Work in ss and inc 1 st each end of needle every 1¼ ins until 66 (70-76) sts. Work straight to 17½ (18-18½) ins from the bottom.

Armhole: Bind off 2 (2-3) sts beg of next 2 rows. Work 0 (2-2) rows even. Dec 1 st each end of needle every other row until 2 sts remain. Bind off. Sew sleeves into body. Sew sleeve and side seams.

Crew neck: With right side facing you and dp needles, pick up approximately 70 (72-72) sts around neck. Rib in k 1, p 1 for 1 in. Bind off *loosely* in ribbing.

V-neck: With right side facing you and dp needles, pick up 24 (26-28) sts across the back neck, and approximately 47 (49-51) sts on each front. Place a ring marker on the needle at the V. Rib in k 1, p 1 to 2 sts before the marker. K 2 tog, sl the marker, sl 1, k 1, psso. Complete the round in k 1, p 1. Rep the round for 1 in. Bind off loosely in ribbing.

Be A Knit Whiz...

Learn to make good seams

Some knitters try to avoid seams by knitting on circular needles. While circular knitting has its place in some designs and with certain types of necklines, every knitter should learn to make good straight seams.

If you're fussy about how your garment drapes, you'll be unhappy with seamless garments. They sometimes look barrel-shaped or spiraled.

Keep your seams elastic—don't pull the stitches too tight.

Utterly simple, fantastically handsome...

Pullover Set-in Sleeve Sweater

There are times when a warm, classic pullover sweater is just the thing to beat the cold. This one's as easy to make as it is to look at. Our pattern makes this sweater as good-looking as the classic pullover shown on page 66 of our tots and teens' section. In crew and v-neck styles.

Yarn: Worsted Weight 20 (24-24) oz.
Blocked Measurement: 38 (42-46) inches for sweater at chest.
Gauge: In stockinette stitch (ss) 4½ stitches (sts) per inch.
Needles: Single point No. 6 and No. 9 or as needed to reach proper gauge. Double point No. 6.
Accessories: 2 st holders.

BACK

Cast on 86 (94-104) sts with smaller sp needles. Rib in k 1, p 1 for 2½ ins. Change to larger needles and continue in ss straight to 16 ins from the bottom of the ribbing. Blocked measurement: 19 (21-23) ins across.

Armhole: Bind off 4 (5-5) sts beg of next 2 rows. Dec 1 st every other row at each armhole edge 4 (5-7) times. Continue straight to 9½ (10-10½) ins from bind-off.

Shoulder: Bind off 8 sts beg of next 4 rows and 7 (8-10) sts beg of next 2 rows. Place the balance 24 (26-28) sts on a holder.

FRONT

Crew neck: Same as back to 7 (7½-8) ins above underarm. Place center 14 (16-16) sts on a holder. Attach a 2nd ball of yarn so you can work both sides of the neck at the same time. Dec 1 st at each neck edge every other row 5 (5-6) times. When the armhole measures the same as the back, bind off at

each shoulder 8 sts 2 times and 7 (9-10) sts 1 time.

V-neck: Same as back to underarm. Divide the sts evenly, attaching a 2nd ball of yarn so you can work both sides at the same time. Dec 1 st at each neck edge every 5 rows 12 (13-14) times. When armhole is same length as back, bind off at each shoulder 8 sts 2 times and 7 (8-10) sts 1 time.

SLEEVES (Make 2)

Cast on 44 (44-46) sts on smaller needles. Rib in k 1, p 1 for 2½ ins. Change to larger needles and inc 6 sts evenly across row. Work in ss and inc 1 st at each end of needle every 1¼ ins until 68 (70-74) sts. Work straight to 17½ (18-18½) ins from the bottom of ribbing.

Armhole: Bind off 4 (5-5) sts beg of next 2 rows. Dec 1 st each end of needle every other row for 5 (5½-6) ins. Bind off 2 sts beg of next 4 rows. Bind off balance.

Finishing: Sew shoulder seams, sleeve and side seams. Insert sleeves into armholes.

Crew neck: With right side facing you and dp needles, pick up 70 (72-74) sts around neck. Rib in k 1, p 1 for 1 in. Bind off *loosely* in ribbing.

V-neck: With right side facing you and dp needles, pick up 24 (26-28) sts across back of neck and approximately 47 (49-51) sts on each front. Place a ring marker on the needles at the V. Rib in k 1, p 1 to 2 sts before the marker, k 2 tog, sl the marker, sl 1, k 1, psso; complete the round in k 1, p 1. Rep this round for 1 in. Bind off *loosely* in ribbing.

Knit-Picking...

Let it dry

Never stretch the ribbing on a garment when you are pinning it down for blocking. Always leave the garment on the board until dry.

Aran Ama (see page 48)   The Westerner

Great to look at, super to wear...

The Westerner

Deck your favorite guy out in this extra-warm pullover, shown on the right above. Its double cable is flanked with a rope stitch for a corded look. And the same pattern is modified for the sleeves...with a twisted knit stitch to pull it all together.

Yarn: Bulky 28 (30-32) oz.
Blocked Measurement: 38 (42-46) inches for sweater at chest.
Gauge: In stockinette stitch (ss) 3½ stitches per inch, 5 rows per inch.

CONTINUED ON NEXT PAGE

CONTINUED FROM PREVIOUS PAGE

Needles: Single point No. 7 and No. 10 or as required to reach proper gauge. Double point No. 7.

BACK

Cast on 68 (74-80) sts using smaller needles. Rib in k 1, p 1 for 2 ins. Change to larger needles. Continue in ss straight to 16 ins from bottom of ribbing. Width: 19 (21-23) ins.

Armhole: Bind off 2 sts beg of next 2 rows. Work 4 rows even. Fashion raglan dec as follows:

Row 1: K 2, sl 1, k 1 psso, k to last 4 sts, k 2 tog, k 2.
Row 2: P.

Rep these two rows until 18 (20-22) sts are left. Place on holder.

FRONT

Cast on 68 (74-80) sts using smaller needle. Rib as for back. Inc 1 st at end of last row. Change to larger needles and continue in ss and pattern as shown below:

Row 1: K 20 (23-26), p 1, k next 2 sts tog but do not remove from left hand needle, k the first of these two sts and remove both from left needle (rope st), p 1, rope, p 2, k 6, p 1, k 6, p 2, rope, p 1, rope, p 1, k 20 (23-26).
Row 2: P 20 (23-26), k 1, p 2, k 1, p 2, k 2, p 6, k 1, p 6, k 2, p 2, k 1, p 2, k 1, p 20 (23-26).
Row 3: K 20 (23-26), p 1, rope, p 1, rope, p 2, sl next 3 sts to dp needle and hold in back, k next 3 sts, k 3 from dp needle, p 1, sl next 3 sts to dp needle and hold in front, k 3, k 3 from dp needle (double cable twist), p 2, rope, p 1, rope, p 1, k 20 (23-26).
Row 4: And all even rows, same as row 2.

Rows 5, 7, 9, 11, 13, 15, 17: Same as row 1.
Row 18: Same as row 2.
Rep rows 3-18 until piece measures 16 ins from bottom of ribbing.

Armhole: Bind off 2 sts at beg of next 2 rows. Fashion the raglan same as on back. When armholes measure 7 (7½-8) ins from underarm, place center 13 (15-17) sts on holder. Working both sides of neck at the same time, and with 2 balls of yarn, dec 1 st at each neck edge every other row 3 times. Continue raglan dec until 2 sts are left. Fasten off.

SLEEVES (Make 2)

Cast on 32 (34-36) sts using smaller needles. Rib in k 1, p 1 for 2½ ins. Change to larger needles and inc 3 (4-5) sts evenly across row. Work in pattern st as follows:

Row 1: *K 2, p 1, rep from * ending k 2 (wrong side).
Row 2: *P 2, k next st through back, rep from * ending p 2.

Rep these two rows of pattern st inc 1 st each end of needle every 1½ ins until 53 (56-61) sts. Be sure to work pattern st into inc areas. Continue straight to 18 (18-19) ins from bottom of ribbing (cuff). Width: 15 (16-17½) ins.

Armhole: Bind off 2 sts beg of next 2 rows. Work 4 rows even. Dec 1 st each end of needle every face row until 3 (2-3) sts remain. Bind off.

NECKLINE

Sew sleeves into body. With dp needles and right side of sweater facing you, pick up 58 (58-60) sts around neck including sts on holders. Work in k 1, p 1 rib for 2 ins. Bind off *loosely* in ribbing.

Sew sleeves and side seams. Block to size. Turn neck in half to inside and tack in place.

Plenty of good-looks in a sweater as warm as a log on the hearth...

Aran Ama

There's nothing better than a sweater as big on comfort and styling as it is on warmth. This thick, bulky, zippered jacket (at left on previous page) has plenty of variation in the stitches, yet it is still easy to knit.

Yarn: Bulky 34 (38-40) oz.
Blocked Measurement: 40 (42-45) inches for sweater at chest.

Gauge: In stockinette stitch (ss) 3½ stitches (sts) per inch.

Needles: Straight No. 9 and No. 10½ or as needed to reach proper gauge.

Accessories: Double point needles or cable needles. St holders.

Note: Be sure to practice the following design patterns before starting sweater.

DESIGN PANELS

Each of the following four Aran patterns will form the design on the garment you will be knitting. Also shown is the twist rib that will be used at the bottom of the back and front as well as on the cuffs of the sleeves.

Pattern A: 3-Twist Mock Cable
Row 1: (Wrong side): P 3.
Row 2: K 3.
Row 3: P 3.
Row 4: K into 3rd st on left-hand needle, then into 2nd st, then into 1st st, then slide them off tog.
Rep rows 1-4.

Pattern B: Double Moss
Row 1: (Wrong side): K 1, p 1.
Row 2: Work sts as you see them.
Row 3: P 1, k 1.
Row 4: Work sts as you see them.
Rep rows 1-4.

Pattern C: Eccentric Cable
Row 1: (Wrong side): P 6.
Row 2: K 6.
Row 3: P 6.
Row 4: Sl next 3 sts to dp needle and hold in back, k next 3 sts, k 3 from dp needle.
Rows 5, 7, 9: Same as row 3.
Rows 6, 8: Same as row 2.
Row 10: Same as row 4.
Rows 11, 13, 15, 17, 19, 21: Same as row 3.
Rows 12, 14, 16, 18, 20: Same as row 2.
Row 22: Same as row 4.
Rep rows 5-22 in above order.

Pattern D: Honey-comb (Multiple of 8 sts)
Row 1: (Wrong side): P 24.
Row 2: *Sl next 2 sts to dp needle and hold in back, k next 2 sts, k 2 from dp needle (BT), sl next 2 sts to dp needle and hold in front, k next 2 sts, k 2 from dp needle (FT), rep from * 2 times more.
Row 3: P 24.
Row 4: K 24.
Row 5: P 24.
Row 6: *FT, BT, rep from * 2 times more.
Row 7: P 24.

Row 8: K 24.
Row 9: P 24.
Rep sequence of rows 2-9 in above order.

Twist Rib: (Used in place of standard ribbing)
Row 1: (Wrong side): *K 1 in back of st (k 1B), p 1, rep from * across row.
Row 2: And all other rows: Same as row 1.

SWEATER

BACK
Cast on 68 (74-80) sts using smaller needles. Twist rib for 2½ ins inc 12 (10-10) sts evenly across last row. Change to larger needles and work all aran patterns shown below.

Note: Since each pattern has a different number of rows in its rep sequence, each pattern will form its own panel. You will be able to follow the sequence of rows in each panel while working the entire back of the sweater. To start the design, work the rows as shown:

Row 1: (Wrong side): K 1, *pattern A* over next 3 sts, *pattern B* over next 6 (7-10) sts, *pattern C* over next 6 sts, k 1, *pattern C*, k 1 (2-2), *pattern D* over next 32 sts, k 1, (2-2), *pattern C*, k 1, *pattern C*, *pattern B* over next 6 (7-10) sts, *pattern A* over next 3 sts, k 1.

Row 2: Working 2nd row of each aran pattern: P 1, *pattern A*, *pattern B*, *pattern C*, p 1, *pattern C*, p 1 (2-2), *pattern D*, p 1 (2-2), *pattern C*, p 1, *pattern C*, *pattern B*, *pattern A*, p 1.

Continue in this manner following the pattern rows for each aran panel working the in-between st as above (k sts on wrong side, p sts on right side). When piece measures 16 ins from bottom of twist ribbing, start armhole. Width of piece, blocked measurement: 20 (21-22½)ins.

Armhole: Bind off 4 sts beg of next 2 rows. Dec 1 st every other row at each armhole edge 6 times. Continue straight to 9½ (10-10½)ins from bind-off row.

Shoulder: Bind off 9 sts beg of next 2 rows and 9½ (10-12) sts beg of next 2 rows. Place balance of 24 (26-28) sts on a holder.

RIGHT FRONT
Cast on 38 (40-44) sts using smaller needle. Twist rib for 2½ ins. Keeping 6 sts next to center edge in twist rib, inc 8 (8-7) sts evenly across balance of last row. Change to larger needles and establish aran design panels.

CONTINUED ON NEXT PAGE

49

CONTINUED FROM PREVIOUS PAGE

Row 1: (Wrong side): K 1, *pattern A, pattern B, pattern C*, k 1, *pattern C*, k 1 (2-2), *pattern D* over next 16 sts, twist rib 6.

Row 2: Twist rib 6, *pattern D*, p 1 (2-2) *pattern C*, p 1, *pattern C, pattern B, pattern A*, p 1.

Continue with pattern panels as on back working in-between sts in same manner. When piece measures the same as on the back, start armhole. Blocked width of front piece: 11½ (12-12¾) ins.

Armhole: Bind off 4 sts at armhole edge. Dec 1 st at armhole edge every other row 6 times. Continue straight to 7 (7½-8) ins from bind-off row. Start neck: At center edge, place 13 (14-15) sts on a holder. Dec 1 st at neck edge every other row 5 times. When armhole measures same as on back, bind off at shoulder edge 9 sts 1 time and 9 (10-12) sts 1 time.

LEFT FRONT

Same as right front but reverse shaping and reverse aran pattern placement.

SLEEVES (Make 2)

Cast on 34 (34-36) sts using smaller needles. Twist rib for 2 ins inc 8 sts evenly across last row. Change to larger needles and establish aran design panels.

Aran Design: Work all pattern panels simultaneously as on back following row sequence for each panel as you work, like this:

Row 1: (Wrong side): *Pattern B* over first 2 (2-3) sts, *pattern C*, k 1, *pattern D* over 24 sts, k 1, *pattern C, pattern B* over last 2 (2-3) sts.

Row 2: *Pattern B, pattern C*, p 1, *pattern D*, p 1, *pattern C, pattern B*.

Continue work sequence of rows for each pattern panel, working in-between sts as on back; at same time inc 1 st each end of needle every 1½ (1¼-1) ins, working additional sts into *pattern B*. When you have 58 (60-64) sts on needle work straight to 17½ (17½-18) ins from bottom of twist rib. Blocked width of piece: 14½ (15-16) ins.

Armhole: Bind off 4 sts beg of next 2 rows. Dec 1 st each end of needle every other row for 5 (5½-6) ins. Bind off 2 sts beg of next 4 rows. Bind off balance.

ASSEMBLY AND FINISHING

Sew shoulder seams.

Neckline: With right side facing you and using smaller needles, pick up approximately 72 (76-80) sts around neck. Twist rib for 4 ins. Bind off *loosely* in ribbing.

Sew side and sleeve seams. Insert sleeves, *stretching sleeve cap* to fit smoothly into armhole.

Face front edges with preshrunk grosgrain ribbon, going from bottom of jacket to half way up neck ribbing. Turn neck ribbing in half to inside of jacket and tack down. Insert zipper up front of jacket.

Be A Knit Whiz...

Making a swatch

Take some of the yarn you plan to use. Take the larger needle given in the pattern and cast on 4 inches at the gauge specified.

For greater accuracy, these patterns show gauge in stockinette stitch. Make your swatch by knitting 1 row, then purling 1 row for 2 inches.

Now measure your swatch. With the knitting still on the needle, place the swatch on a hard, smooth surface and press the swatch flat with a hard ruler *(without stretching the knitting)*.

If it is less than 4 inches wide, your gauge is too tight. Increase the size of the needle one size and try another two inches in stockinette stitch. If the swatch is more than 4 inches wide, your gauge is too loose.

If your swatch is a quarter inch off size at this point, your finished garment *could be anywhere from 1½ to 3 inches off size when completed!*

If you can't adjust your gauge after using two other needle sizes, try switching from metal to plastic needles, or vice-versa. Or try a different yarn—sometimes boucle, hairy or textured yarns give knitters problems.

"Swatch" to the right needles

What drives a yarn shop operator to the looney bin is the customer who insists on using a large needle with fine yarns. Or a fine needle with bulky yarns just because that's the needle she has handy at home.

GAUGE is the key to successful knitting. Not needle size, not yarn ply, but *GAUGE.* Every pattern in this book was designed with a particular gauge. If you stay on gauge, your garment will be the proper size when finished.

Some knitters have natural gauge just like some vocalists have natural pitch. Other knitters have problems. But with care, knitting problems can be overcome.

Make a sample swatch with the yarn you'll be using, so you can measure your knitting gauge per inch to see if it corresponds with the gauge required in the pattern.

If you're a loose knitter and you don't take time for this little exercise, you might end up with a sweater that looks like this.

And if you're a tight knitter, you could end up with a garment that looks like this.

Be A Knit Whiz...

Take a little time out

If your knitting problems don't clear up after dropping several needle sizes and trying a different kind of yarn, perhaps you should take some time to retrain your fingers.

Knit a scarf 50-60 inches long, concentrating on firmly knitting and purling each stitch. This is helpful, too, if your knitting is "striped" because your knit row is tighter than your purl row.

Some knitters use a smaller needle on the purl row. Others work to retrain their fingers to avoid the confusion of two different sized needles.

A great, traditional style with appeal for all time...

Snow King Pullover

Our thick, three-cabled sweater is so warm and masculine, it looks right at home on the farm, at the supermarket or on the ski slope. This toasty turtleneck is also fun to make!

Yarn: Bulky 28 (30-32) oz.
Blocked Measurement: 38 (42-46) inches for sweater at chest.
Gauge: In stockinette stitch (ss) 3½ stitches (sts) per inch.
Needles: Single point No. 8 and No. 10½ or as needed to reach proper gauge. Double point No. 8 and No. 10.
Accessories: St holders.

BACK
Cast on 68 (74-80) sts using smaller needle. Rib in k 1, p 1 for 2 ins. Change to larger needles. Continue straight in ss to 15 ins from bottom of ribbing. Check width: 19 (21-23) ins.

Armhole: Bind off 3 (3-4) sts beg of next 2 rows. Dec 1 st each end of needle every other row 3 (4-4) times. Work straight until piece measures 9½ (10-10½) ins above underarm.

Shoulder: Bind off 9 (10-12) sts beg of next 2 rows and 9 sts beg of next 2 rows. Place balance 20 (22-22) sts on a holder.

FRONT
Cast on 68 (74-80) sts using smaller needle. Rib in k 1, p 1 for 2 ins, inc 10 sts evenly across last row of ribbing. Change to larger needles. Continue in following pattern:
Row 1:   K 22 (25-28), p 4, k 6, p 4, k 6, p 4, k 6, p 4, k 22 (25-28).
Row 2:   P 22 (25-28), k 4, p 6, k 4, p 6, k 4, p 6, k 4, p 22 (25-28).
Row 3:   K 22 (25-28), p 4, sl next 3 sts to dp needle and hold in front, k next 3, k 3 from dp needle (cable made), p 4, cable, p 4, cable, p 4, k 22 (25-28).

Rows 4, 6, 8, 10, 12: Same as row 2.
Rows 5, 7, 9, 11: Same as row 1.
Rep rows 3 through 12 for cable pattern. When piece measures 16 ins from bottom of ribbing, start armholes. Check width: 19 (21-23) ins.

Armhole: Bind off 3 (3-4) sts beg of next 2 rows. Dec 1 st each end of needle every other row 4 (5-5) times. Work straight until piece measures 7 (7½-8) ins above underarm. *Start neck:* Work across 24 (25-28) sts. Place next 16 (18-18) sts on a holder. Attach a second ball and complete the row. Work this with 2 balls of yarn: Dec 1 st on each side of this neck opening every other row 4 times. Continue straight until armhole is same as back.

Shoulder: Bind off 10 (11-13) sts once and 10 sts once on each shoulder.

SLEEVES (Make 2)
Cast on 32 (34-36) sts using smaller needles. Rib in k 1, p 1 for 2 ins inc 4 sts evenly across last row of ribbing. Change to larger needles. Work in ss, inc 1 st each end of needle every 1½ ins until there are 52 (56-60) sts on needle. Continue straight to 18 (18½-19) ins from bottom of ribbing. Check width: 15 (16-17) ins.

Armhole: Bind off 3 (3-4) sts beg of next 2 rows. Dec 1 st each end of needle every other row for 5 (5½-6) ins. Bind off 2 sts beg of next 2 rows. Bind off balance.

FINISHING
Sew shoulder seams, side and sleeve seams. Insert sleeves into armholes.

Neck: With right side facing you, using No. 8 dp needle, pick up approximately 56 (56-58) sts around neck including sts on holders. Rib in k 1, p 1 for 3 ins. Change to No. 10 dp needle and continue for 4 ins more. Bind off *loosely* in ribbing.

Look every bit a gentleman in this casual, comfortable sweater...

Indian Summer

A trim, man's fashion must, with a masculine three color mosaic pattern. This sweater jacket has a tweed front and back, plus hemmed bottom, for a really versatile style.

Yarn: Worsted Weight: 16 (16-16) oz Main Color (MC). 4 (8-8) oz Contrast Colors A and B.

Blocked Measurement: 38 (42-46) inches for sweater at chest.

Gauge: In stockinette stitch (ss) 4½ stitches (sts) per inch, 6 rows per inch.

Needles: Single point No. 6, No. 8 and No. 9 or as needed to reach proper gauge.

Accessories: 3 st holders
              1 yarn bobbin.

Pattern Stitch: Row 1: Color A, (right side), *k 1, sl 1, rep from * across row.
Row 2: Color A, p.
Row 3: Color B, *sl 1, k 1; rep from * across row.
Row 4: Color B, p.
Rows 5 and 6: MC, k.
Rep these 6 rows for color pattern.

BACK
With MC, cast on 88 (94-104) sts using No. 8 needle. Work in ss for 1 in. K 1 row on the p side (hem row). Change to No. 9 needles and continue in pattern st straight to 16 ins from the hem row.

Armhole: Bind off 2 (2-3) sts beg of next 2 rows. Work 2 (2-0) rows even. Dec 1 st every other row at each armhole edge until 24 (26-28) sts remain. Bind off.

FRONT SECTIONS
The fronts are worked in the same pattern st, and the bands are worked in the MC. To do this, a ball of MC *and* a bobbin of MC for the band will be needed. As you come to the band, drop the strand you have been using and bring the bobbin thread around the dropped strand so as not to leave a hole.

RIGHT FRONT
With MC cast on 44 (48-51) sts using No. 8 needle. Work in ss for 1 in. Make a hem row. Change to No. 9 needles and cast on 13 sts at the center front edge. Knit these sts this way: K 6, sl 1, k 6 in MC, and work the balance in the pattern st as for the back. Continue as established to 16 ins from the hem row.

Armhole: Bind off 2 (3-3) sts at armhole edge. Dec 1 st at the same edge every other row as for the back. *At the same time the armholes are started, start the v-neck.* Do all neck dec just inside the front band. Dec 1 st every 5th row 11 (12-13) times. Continue the raglan until only the 13 border sts are left. Continue on these for another 2½ ins. Bind off.

LEFT FRONT
Same as the right but reverse the shaping and remember to use a bobbin for the front band.

SLEEVES (Make 2)
With MC cast on 44 (44-46) sts, using No. 6 needle. Rib in k 1, p 1 for 2 ins. Change to No. 9 needles and inc 4 sts evenly across the needle. Work in ss and inc 1 st each end of needle every 1 in until 68 (70-76) sts. Continue straight to 17½ (18-18½) ins from the bottom.

Armhole: Bind off 2 sts beg of next 2 rows. Dec 1 st each end of needle on every other row until 2 sts remain. Bind off.

FINISHING
Sew in sleeves. Sew side and sleeve seam. Join the neck band and attach it to the back neck of the sweater. Turn up the bottom hem and tack down. Turn back the facing and tack it down, putting a preshrunk grosgrain ribbon between the facing and the sweater on the fronts up to the V. Make machine buttonholes and sew on buttons.

Look like you haven't a care in the world...

Big Leaguer

Here's a unique short-sleeved cardigan with a mosaic pattern any man will love to wear. The straight hemmed bottom is flattering to men with both slim and large builds.

Yarn: Sportsweight 12 (14-16) oz Main Color (MC). 2 (2-2) oz Colors A and B.
Blocked Measurement: 38 (42-46) inches for sweater at chest.
Gauge: In stockinette stitch (ss) 5½ stitches (sts) per inch.
Needles: Single point No. 4, No. 5 and No. 6.
Accessories: 3 st holders.

PATTERN STITCH
Rows 1 and 3: MC—k.
Rows 2 and 4: MC—p.
Rows 5 and 6: Color A—k.
Row 7: Color B—k 1, *sl 1 with yarn in back, k 1; rep from * across row.
Row 8: Color B—k 1, *sl 1 with yarn in front, k 1; rep from * across row.
Rows 9 and 10: Color A—k.
Rep these 10 rows for color pattern.

BACK
With MC cast on 105 (117-127) sts with No. 5 needles. Work in ss for 1¼ ins. K 1 row in p side (hem row). Change to No. 6 needles and continue in ss straight to 15 ins from the hem row.

Armhole: Bind off 6 sts beg of next 2 rows. Dec 1 st every other row at each armhole edge 5 (6-8) times. Continue straight to 9½ (10-10½) ins from bind-off.

Shoulder: Bind off 8 (10-10) sts beg of next 4 rows and 9 (10-12) sts beg of next 2 rows. Bind off balance—33 (33-35) sts.

FRONTS
The fronts are worked in pattern st, and the bands are worked in the MC. To do this: You will need a ball of MC and a bobbin of MC for the band. As you come to the band, drop the strand you have been working with and bring the bobbin thread around the dropped strand, so you won't leave a hole.

RIGHT FRONT
With MC cast on 51 (57-61) sts with No. 5 needles. Work in ss for 1¼ ins. Make a hem row. Change to No. 6 needles and cast on 15 sts at the center edge. Work these sts like this: K 7, sl 1, k 7 in MC and work the pattern st on the balance. Continue as established to 15 ins from the hem row.

Armhole: Bind off 6 sts at the armhole edge. Dec 1 st at the same edge every other row 5 (6-8) times. At the same time as the armhole is begun, start the v-neck. Do all neck dec just inside the border sts. Dec 1 st every 4 (4-5) rows 15 times. When armhole is the same length as the back, bind off for shoulder 8 (10-10) sts twice and 9 (10-12) sts 1 time. Continue on the 15 border sts for another 2½ ins.

LEFT FRONT
Same as the right front but reverse the shaping and see the note on the fronts.

SLEEVES (Make 2)
With MC cast on 66 (70-76) sts with No. 4 needles. Rib in k 1, p 1 for 1½ ins. Change to No. 6 needles and inc 6 sts evenly across row. Work in ss and inc 1 st each end of needle every 1 in to 82 (86-92) sts. Work straight to 8 ins from the bottom of the ribbing.

Armhole: Bind off 6 sts beg of next 2 rows. Dec 1 st each end of needle every other row for 5 (5½-6) ins. Bind off 2 sts beg of next 4 rows. Bind off balance.

FINISHING
Sew shoulder seams, sleeve seams and side seams. Insert sleeves into armholes. Join the neck band and attach it to the back of the sweater. Turn up the hem at the bottom. Turn back the front and neck facing and insert a preshrunk grosgrain ribbon between the facing and the front. Make machine buttonholes and sew on buttons.

A traditional style with a sporty new twist...

Tattersall Vest

The emphasis on good-looking geometrics is unmistakable with this popular man's cardigan sweater vest. Contrasting lines are easy to do, and the hemmed bottom makes a trim-looking fit for any man.

Yarn: Sportsweight 10 (12-14) oz Main Color (MC). 1 (1-1) oz each of Contrast Colors A and B.
Blocked Measurement: 38 (42-46) inches for vest at chest.
Gauge: In stockinette stitch (ss) 5½ stitches (sts) per inch.
Needles: Single point No. 5 and No. 6 or as needed to reach proper gauge. Double point No. 5.

BACK
Cast on 105 (115-125) sts with the smaller needle. K in ss for 1 in. K 1 row in the p side (hem row). Change to the larger needles and continue in pattern st this way:
Row 1: K 2, *p 1, k 9, rep from * across row, end p 1, k 2.
Row 2: P.
Rep these two rows for 1 in. Starting the next k row working always in the established pattern, work 1 row with color A, 9 rows MC, 1 row color B, 9 rows MC, 1 row color A, etc., alternating the colors throughout the garment. At 16 ins start the armhole.

Armhole: Bind off 8 sts beg of next 2 rows. Dec 1 st every other row at each armhole edge 6 (9-10) times. Continue straight to 9 (9½-10) ins from bind-off.

Shoulder: Bind off 6 sts beg of next 4 rows, 5 (6-7) sts beg of next 2 rows, and 5 (6-8) sts beg of next 2 rows. Bind off the balance 33 (33-35) sts.

RIGHT FRONT
Cast on 51 (57-61) sts with smaller needle. K in ss for 1 in. Make a hem row. Change to larger needles and cast on 15 sts at the front edge. Work the pattern st like this:
Row 1: K 7, sl 1, *k 9, p 1; rep from * across row, end k 8 (4-8).
Row 2: P.
Work the color pattern as on the back. Be sure to carry the color stripe through the front facing band. When the front measures 16 ins from the hem row, start the armhole.

Armhole: Bind off 9 sts at the armhole edge. Dec 1 st at the same edge every other row 6 (9-10) times. At the same time the armhole is started, start the V-neck. Do all dec at 8 sts inside the sl st edge. Dec 1 st every 5th row 14 (15-15) times. When armhole measures the same as the back, bind off for the shoulders the same as the back: 6 sts twice, 5 (6-7) sts once, and 5 (6-8) sts once. Continue on the 15 border sts for another 2½ ins. Bind off.

LEFT FRONT
Same as the right front but reverse the shaping and be sure to *reverse the placement of the st pattern.*

FINISHING
Using the colors A and B alternately, and with crochet hook, sl st the vertical rows using the p st to keep the lines straight. Sew side and shoulder seams. Turn up bottom hem. Join the neck band across and attach one edge to the back neck of sweater.

Armholes: With right sides facing you and using dp needles, pick up approximately 97 (103-108) sts around the armhole. Work 1 row of p; then continue in k for 1 in. Bind off loosely. Turn to inside and tack in place.

Turn back the facing on the fronts and neck. Put a preshrunk grosgrain ribbon between the facing and front up to the point where the V begins. Tack entire facing in place. Make machine buttonholes. Sew on buttons.

Big on comfort, with an easy-going look…

Swagger Jacket

This handsome jacket sweater makes an identical twin to our women's swagger jacket on page 33. Both of you should look great in them!

Yarn: Bulky 21 (22) 2 oz balls, or in knitting worsted weight (used double strand), 10 (11) 4 oz balls.
Blocked Measurement: 46 (48) inches for sweater at chest.
Gauge: In stockinette stitch (ss) 3½ stitches (sts) per inch, 5 rows per inch.
Needles: No. 10 and No. 10½ or as needed to reach proper gauge. 29 inch No. 10 circular needle.

BACK
Cast on 78 (80) sts with smaller needles. Rib in k 2, p 2 for 1½ ins. Change needles. Continue in ss straight to 17 ins from bottom.

Armhole: Bind off 2 sts beg of next 2 rows. Work 2 rows even. Dec 1 st each end of needle every other row like this: K 2, p 2 tog, k to last 4 sts, p 2 tog, k 2. P the next row. Rep last 2 rows until 20 sts remain. Bind off.

RIGHT FRONT
Cast on 42 (46) sts with smaller needle. Rib in k 2, p 2 for 1½ ins. Change to larger needles and continue in ss to 17 ins from bottom. Mark one edge for armhole and one for neck.

Armhole: Bind off 2 sts at armhole edge and dec 1 st at neck edge. Work 2 rows even. Dec 1 st at armhole edge every other row in the same fashion as for the back. Rep neck dec every 4th row 11 (14) times more. Continue raglan to 2 sts. Bind off.

LEFT FRONT
Same as right front but reverse shaping.

SLEEVES (Make 2)
Cast on 46 (48) sts on smaller needle. Rib in k 2, p 2

for 1½ ins. Change needles and work in ss. Inc 1 st each end of needle every 2 ins until 58 (60) sts. Continue straight to 17 ins from bottom.

Armhole: Bind off 2 sts beg of next 2 rows. Work 4 rows even. Dec 1 st each end of needle every other row in same fashion as for the back. When 2 sts remain, bind off.

Sew in sleeves. Sew body and sleeve seams.

COLLAR
Cast on 234 (238) sts on circular needle. Work in k 2, p 2 for 8 rows. Bind off 56 sts beg of next 2 rows, 2 sts beg of next 12 (14) rows, 7 sts beg of next 6 rows, 8 sts beg of next 4 rows. Bind off balance 24 sts.

POCKETS (Make 2)
Cast on 26 sts with smaller needle. Rib in k 2, p 2, for 7 ins. Bind off.

BELT
Cast on 14 sts using smaller needle. *K 1, yarn forward, sl 1 as to p; rep from * across row. Work all rows alike. Make belt 50 ins long or as desired.

FINISHING
Attach collar to jacket, using the bound-off edge of the collar as the seam edge, as follows: (1) Tack center point of bound-off edge of collar to center point of back of neck; (2) tack ends of collar piece to the respective front edges at the bottom of the jacket; (3) the points at which the collar starts inc in width should be tacked to the points at which the front edges of the jacket start the V-neck dec. Complete sewing collar to jacket, easing the seam around the front edges and neckline so it lays smoothly.

Place pockets at bottom of fronts in positions most comfortable to you.

Make belt loops by sc leftover yarn.

Sierra Tunic (see page 85)   **Man's Pullover Vest**   **Autumn Haze** (see page 11)

Add a gentlemanly finish to any outfit…

Man's Pullover Vest

This lightweight vest, made in either v-neck or crew neck styles,
is perfect for dressing up any casual wear. Or, shut out drafts in a chilly
office with this fashion extra worn with a favorite suit and tie.
Vests can add a real dapper look to everything your favorite man owns.

Yarn: Sportsweight 8 (10-12) oz.
Blocked Measurement: 38 (42-46) inches for vest at chest.
Gauge: In stockinette stitch (ss) 5½ stitches (sts) per inch.
Needles: No. 3, No. 6 or as needed to reach proper gauge. Double point No. 4.
Accessories: 2 st holders.

BACK

Cast on 104 (116-126) sts using smaller needle. Rib in k 1, p 1 for 2½ ins. Change to larger needles and continue straight in ss to 15 ins from bottom of ribbing. Blocked measurement of piece: 19 (21-23) ins.

Armhole: Bind off 6 sts beg of next 2 rows. Dec 1 st every other row at each armhole edge 10 (12-14) times. Continue straight to 9½ (10-10½) ins from bind-off row.

Shoulder: Bind off 7 sts beg of next 4 rows, and 6 (10-12) sts beg of next 2 rows. Place balance of 32 (32-34) sts on a holder.

FRONT

Crew Neck: Same as back to 7 (7½-8) ins above underarm. Place center 20 (20-22) sts on a holder. Attach a 2nd ball of yarn at other side of holder so you can work both sides of neck on each row. Continue in ss, dec 1 st at each neck edge 6 times. Continue straight until armhole measures same as on back. Bind off 7 sts 2 times at each shoulder edge, then 6 (10-12) sts at each shoulder edge 1 time.

V-neck: Same as back to underarm. Divide sts evenly attaching a 2nd ball of yarn. Working both sides on each row, and working armhole edges as on back, dec 1 st at each neck edge every 4 (5-5) rows 16 (16-17) times. Continue straight until armhole measures same as on back, then bind off 7 sts at each shoulder edge 2 times, and 6 (10-12) sts 1 time.

FINISHING

Sew shoulder seams.

Crew neck: With right side facing you and with dp needles, pick up approximately 90 (90-92) sts around neck edge. Rib in k 1, p 1 for 2 ins. Bind off loosely in ribbing. Turn half of ribbing to inside and tack down.

V-neck: With right side facing you and with dp needles, pick up 32 (32-34) sts across back of neck and approximately 57 (60-62) sts on each front. Place a marker on needle at the V. Rib in k 1, p 1 to 2 sts before marker, k 2 tog, sl marker, sl 1, k 1, psso, complete round in rib, rep the dec on each side of marker every row for 1 in. Then continue in rib but inc 1 st on each side of marker for another in. Bind off loosely in ribbing. Turn half of ribbing to inside and tack down.

Both styles: Sew side seams.

Armhole bands: With right side facing you and using dp needles, pick up approximately 104 (110-116) sts around armhole. Rib in k 1, p 1 for 2 ins. Bind off loosely in ribbing. Turn half of ribbing to inside and tack down.

Knit-Picking...

Give it the professional look

Blocking is the final step in knitting to give a smooth, professional finish to your handmade garment.

Only wool garments should be blocked–and then only after the garment has been assembled.

Place a clean white towel on a rug or large board. Pat the garment into shape and pin in place with stainless steel T-pins.

Steam with an iron, *but be sure not to let the iron touch the garment.* Never block heavily since it's not a good idea and not necessary.

Synthetics lose their resilience and soft, airy qualities if blocked, so don't! Follow the instructions on the yarn label.

If you send a wool or synthetic sweater to the dry cleaners, be sure to label "Do Not Block."

Share a laugh in a relaxed, casual shirt...

String Shirt

Here's a great looking twin to our woman's string shirt on page 32, sure to be a hit with its adjustable sleeves. Wear sleeves up or down, with a shirt underneath, or plain.

Yarn: Sportsweight 16 (18-20) oz.
Blocked Measurement: 38 (40-42-44) inches for shirt at chest.
Gauge: In stockinette stitch (ss) 6 stitches (sts) per inch.
Needles: Single point No. 4 and No. 5.
Accessories: Crochet Hook No. 0 steel 3 st holders.

BACK
Cast on 116 (120-126-132) sts using the smaller needle. Work in ss for 1¼ ins. K 1 row on p side (hem row). Change to larger needles and continue in ss straight to 16 ins from the hem row. Blocked width of piece 19 (20-21-22) ins.

Armhole: Bind off 2 (2-2-3) sts beg of next 2 rows. On the next row change from ss to k 2, p 2 rib. Dec 1 st every other row at each armhole edge until 30 (32-34-36) sts remain. Place on a holder.

FRONT
Same as the back to 1 in above the armhole. Bind off the center 2 sts. Attach a 2nd ball of yarn so you can work both sides of the front at the same time. Continue with the armhole dec until 15 (16-17-18) sts remain on each side. Place them on a holder.

SLEEVES (Make 2)
Cast on 88 (90-94-98) sts using the larger needle. Rib in k 2, p 2 straight to 13 ins from the bottom.

Armhole: Bind off 2 (2-2-3) sts beg of next 2 rows. Dec 1 st each end of needle until 2 sts remain. Bind off.

FINISHING
Sew sleeves into body.

Collar: With *inside* facing, using No. 4 needles, pick up 64 (68-72-76) sts around neck. Keep pattern as established on the fronts and back and adjust the number of sts if necessary so the ribbing sequence is not disrupted. Work in k 2, p 2 for 3½ ins. Bind off in ribbing. Sew side and sleeve seam. Work 2 rows of sc on the two front edges of yoke opening. Lap them at the bottom of the opening and tack them down. Turn up hem at the bottom and tack in place. This shirt looks best when it is pressed quite flat. Use a steam iron and cool setting and proceed with caution.

More sweater fun and a breeze to make...

Pullover Raglan Sleeve Sweater

Use your knitting time wisely by making this great sweater. The child or teen you make it for is sure to choose it as a favorite. Our pattern is a twin to the women's classic raglan pullover, shown on page 8. Real warm and stylish too.

Yarn: Worsted Weight 12 (12-16-16) oz.
Blocked Measurement: 28 (30-32-34) inches for sweater at chest.
Gauge: In stockinette stitch (ss) 4½ stitches (sts) per inch, 6 rows per inch.
Needles: Single point No. 6 and No. 9 or as needed to reach proper gauge. Double point No. 6.
Accessories: 2 st holders.

BACK

Cast on 62 (68-72-76) sts using small sp needle. Rib in k 1, p 1 for 2½ ins. Change to larger needles and continue in ss to 11½ (12-12-13) ins from bottom of ribbing. Blocked measurement: 14 (15-16-17) ins.

Armhole: Bind off 2 sts beg of next 2 rows. Work 2 rows even. Dec 1 st every other row at each armhole edge until 18 (20-20-20) sts remain. Place on a holder.

FRONT

Crew neck: Same as back to 4½ (4½-5¼-5¾) ins above underarm. Place center 12 sts on a holder. Attach a 2nd ball of yarn so you can work each side of neck at the same time. Dec 1 st at each neck edge every other row 3 (4-4-4) times. At the same time continue the raglan dec to 0 sts.

V-neck: Same as back to underarm. At the same time the armhole is started, divide the sts evenly; attach a 2nd ball of yarn and work both sides of the neck at the same time. Dec 1 st at each neck edge every 4 (4-5-5) rows 9 (10-10-10) times. At the same time continue the raglan dec until 0 sts remain.

SLEEVES (Make 2)

Cast on 30 (32-34-34) sts using smaller needles. Rib in k 1, p 1 for 2½ ins. Change to larger needles and inc 4 sts evenly across row. Work in ss and inc 1 st each end of needle every 1½ ins until 48 (50-54-56) sts. Continue straight to 13½ (14½-15½-16½) ins from the bottom of the ribbing.

Armhole: Bind off 2 sts beg of next 2 rows. Work 0 (2-4-4) rows even. Dec 1 st each end of needle every other row until 2 sts remain. Bind off. Sew sleeves into body. Sew sleeve and side seams.

Crew neck: With right side facing you and using dp needles, pick up approximately 52 (60-62-62) sts around neck. Rib in k 1, p 1 for 1 in. Bind off *loosely* in ribbing.

V-neck: With right side facing you and using dp needles, pick up 18 (20-20-20) sts across back neck, and approximately 31 (33-39-41) sts on each front. Place a ring marker on the needles at the V. Rib in k 1, p 1, to 2 sts before the marker. K 2 tog, sl the marker, sl 1, k 1, psso. Complete the round in k 1, p 1 rib. Rep the round for 1 in. Bind off *loosely* in ribbing.

Knit-Picking...

Shop around for help with problems

If you have problems with your knitting techniques, or if you can't hold gauge, try buying your yarn from a yarn shop that gives customer assistance.

A successful garment is well worth the slight extra cost of yarn bought at a knitting specialty shop where you can get help when you have knitting problems.

Happiness is—a classic sweater that looks as good as it feels...

Pullover Set-in Sleeve Sweater

Make the kids happy with a carefree sweater they can wear with everything. Easy to make and fun to wear, this wardrobe basic can be dressed up with pattern stitches and colors any way you want!

Yarn: Worsted Weight 12 (12-16-16) oz.
Blocked Measurement: 28 (30-32-34) inches for sweater at chest.
Gauge: In stockinette stitch (ss) 4½ stitches (sts) per inch.
Needles: Single point No. 6 and No. 9 or as needed to reach proper gauge. Double point No. 6.
Accessories: 2 st holders.

BACK

Cast on 62 (68-72-76) sts using small sp needle. Rib in k 1, p 1 for 2½ ins. Change to larger needles and continue in ss straight to 11½ (12-12-13) ins from bottom of ribbing. Blocked width: 14 (15-16-17) ins.

Armhole: Bind off 3 (3-4-4) sts beg of next 2 rows. Dec 1 st every other row at each armhole edge 2 (3-3-5) times. Continue straight to 6 (6½-7¾-8¼) ins from bind-off.

Shoulder: Bind off 6 sts beg of next 4 rows, 5 (6-7-7) sts beg of next 2 rows. Place balance of 18 (20-20-20) sts on a holder.

FRONT

Crew Neck: Same as back to 4½ (4½-5¼-5¾) ins above underarm. Place center 12 sts on a holder. Attach a 2nd ball of yarn so you can work both sides of the neck at the same time. Dec 1 st at each neck edge every other row 3 (4-4-4) times. When armhole measures same as on back, bind off at each shoulder 6 sts 2 times, and 5 (6-7-7) sts 1 time.

V-Neck: Same as back to underarm. Divide the sts evenly, attaching a 2nd ball of yarn so you can work both sides of neck at the same time. Work armhole edges same as on back, at same time dec 1 st at each neck edge every 4 (4-5-5) rows 9 (10-10-10) times. When armhole is the same length as back, bind off for each shoulder 6 sts 2 times and 5 (6-7-7) sts 1 time.

SLEEVES (Make 2)

Cast on 30 (32-34-36) sts using smaller needles. Rib in k 1, p 1 for 2½ ins. Change to larger needles and inc 4 sts evenly across row. Work in ss and inc 1 st each end of needle every 1 in until 48 (50-54-56) sts. Continue straight to 13½ (14½-15½-16½) ins from bottom of ribbing.

Armhole: Bind off 3 (3-4-4) sts beg of next 2 rows. Dec 1 st each end of needle every other row for 3 (3½-3½-4) ins. Bind off 2 sts beg of next 4 rows. Bind off balance.

FINISHING

Sew shoulder seams, sleeve and side seams. Insert sleeves into armholes.

Crew neck: With right side facing you and using smaller dp needles, pick up approximately 52 (60-62-62) sts around neck. Rib in k 1, p 1 for 1 in. Bind off *loosely* in ribbing.

V-neck: With right side facing you and using smaller dp needles, pick up 18 (20-20-20) sts from back of neck and 31 (33-39-41) sts on each front. Place a ring marker on needle at V. Rib in k 1, p 1 to 2 sts before marker. K 2 tog, sl the marker, skp. Complete the round in k 1, p 1 rib. Rep this row for 1 in. Bind off *loosely* in ribbing.

Dress warm and look sharp in this children's and teen's classic...

Cardigan Set-in Sleeve Sweater

Because you like your family to look terrific and stay warm too, this sweater is perfect to take along in chilly weather. It's a smaller version of our classic cardigan set-in sleeve sweater shown on page 43 of the men's section.

Yarn: Worsted Weight 12 (12-16-16) oz.
Blocked Measurement: 28 (30-32-34) inches for sweater at chest.
Gauge: In stockinette stitch (ss) 4½ stitches (sts) per inch.
Needles: Single point No. 6 and No. 9 or as needed to reach proper gauge.
Accessories: 3 st holders.

BACK
Cast on 62 (68-72-76) sts using smaller needles. Rib in k 1, p 1 for 2½ ins. Change to larger needles and continue in ss straight to 11½ (12-12-13) ins from bottom of ribbing. Blocked measurement: 14 (15-16-17) ins wide.

Armhole: Bind off 3 (3-4-4) sts beg of next 2 rows. Dec 1 st every other row at each armhole edge 2 (3-3-5) times. Continue straight to 6 (6½-7½-8) ins from bind-off.

Shoulder: Bind off 6 sts beg of next 4 rows and 5 (6-7-7) sts beg of next 2 rows. For crew neck, place balance 18 (20-20-20) sts on a holder. For v-neck, bind off.

RIGHT FRONT
Cast on 36 (38-40-42) sts using smaller needles. Rib in k 1, p 1 for 2½ ins. Keeping the center edge 6 sts in k 1, p 1 for the border, change to larger needles and continue in ss to 11½ (12-12-13) ins from the bottom.

Crew neck and armhole: Bind off 3 (3-4-4) sts at armhole edge. Dec 1 st at the same edge every other row 2 (3-3-5) times. Work straight to 4½ (4½-5½-5¾) ins from bind-off. At the center

edge place 10 sts on a holder. Dec 1 st at the same edge every other row 4 times. When armhole measures same as back, bind off at shoulder edge 6 sts 2 times and 5 (6-7-7) sts 1 time.

V-neck and armhole: Bind off 3 (3-4-4) sts at armhole edge. Work to last 8 sts, k 2 tog (neck dec), work border. Continue as established doing all neck dec just inside the 6 border sts. Dec at the armhole edge 1 st every other row 2 (3-3-5) times and at the same time dec at the neck edge 1 st every 5th row 7 times more. When armhole measures same as back, bind off at shoulder edge 6 sts 2 times and 5 (6-7-7) sts 1 time. Continue working border sts for another 2 ins. Bind off.

LEFT FRONT
Same as right but *reverse shaping.* Rib in p 1, k 1.

SLEEVES (Make 2)
Cast on 30 (32-32-34) sts using smaller needles. Rib in k 1, p 1 for 2 ins. Change to larger needles and inc 4 sts evenly across row. Work in ss and inc 1 st each end of needle every 1½ ins until 48 (50-54-56) sts. Continue straight to 13½ (14½-15½-16½) ins from the bottom.

Armhole: Bind off 3 (3-4-4) sts beg of next 2 rows. Dec 1 st each end of needle every other row for 3 (3½-3½-4) ins. Bind off 2 sts beg of next 4 rows. Bind off balance.

FINISHING
Sew shoulder seams, sleeve and side seams. Insert sleeves into armholes.

Crew neck: With right side facing you and smaller needles, pick up 57 (67-73-73) sts around neck. Rib in k 1, p 1 for 1 in. Bind off loosely in ribbing.

V-neck: Join band and attach it to the back neck of sweater.

Face each front to the V with preshrunk grosgrain ribbon and make machine buttonholes. Sew on buttons.

Cardigan Raglan Sleeve Sweater

Cardigans (and especially raglan sleeved ones!) are just right for kids since they can be worn with everything from stretch shirts to ties. Raglan sleeves are comfy even while kids grow. This pattern makes a twin to our raglan sleeve cardigan shown on page 6 of the women's sweater section.

Yarn: Worsted Weight 12 (12-16-16) oz.
Blocked Measurement: 28 (30-32-34) inches for sweater at chest.
Gauge: In stockinette stitch (ss) 4½ stitches (sts) per inch, 6 rows per inch.
Needles: Single point No. 6 and No. 9 or as needed to reach proper gauge.
Accessories: 3 st holders.

BACK

Cast on 62 (68-72-76) sts using the smaller needle. Rib in k 1, p 1 for 2½ ins. Change to larger needles and continue in ss straight to 11½ (12-12-13) ins from the bottom of the ribbing. Blocked measurement should be 14 (15-16-17) ins across.

Armhole: Bind off 2 sts beg of next 2 rows. Work 2 rows even. Dec 1 st every other row at each armhole edge until 18 (20-20-20) sts remain. For crew neck place on a holder. For v-neck, bind off.

RIGHT FRONT

Cast on 36 (38-40-42) sts using smaller needle. Rib in k 1, p 1 for 2½ ins. Keeping the center edge 6 sts in k 1, p 1 for the border, change to larger needles and continue in ss to 11½ (12-12-12) ins from the bottom.

Crew neck and armhole: Bind off 2 sts at armhole edge. Work 2 rows even. Dec 1 st at the same edge every other row as for the back. When the sweater measures 4½ (4½-5½-5¾) ins above the underarm, start neck.

Neckline: At the center edge place 10 sts on a

holder. Dec 1 st at the same edge every other row 4 times. Continue raglan dec to 0 sts.

Neck and armhole: Bind off 2 sts at the armhole edge. Work 2 rows even and then dec raglan the same as on the back. *At the same time as the armhole is started start the v-neck.* Do all neck dec just inside the 6 front border sts. Dec 1 st every 5 rows 8 times. When only the 6 border sts remain, continue for another 2 ins. Bind off.

LEFT FRONT

Same as right front but *reverse shaping.* Rib in p 1, k 1.

SLEEVES (Make 2)

Cast on 30 (32-32-34) sts using smaller needles. Rib in k 1, p 1, for 2 ins. Change to larger needles and inc 4 sts evenly across row. Work in ss and inc 1 st each end of needle every 1½ ins until 48 (50-54-56) sts. Work straight to 13½ (14½-15½-16½) ins from bottom of ribbing.

Armhole: Bind off 2 sts beg of next 2 rows. Work 0 (2-2-4) rows even. Dec 1 st each end of needle every other row until 2 sts remain. Bind off.

Sew in sleeves. Sew side and sleeve seams.

Crew neck: With right side facing you and smaller needles, pick up 57 (67-73-73) sts around neck. Rib in k 1, p 1 for 1 in. Bind off loosely in ribbing.

V-neck: Sew the band together and attach it to the back of the neck of the sweater.

Face each front edge with preshrunk grosgrain ribbon. Make machine buttonholes. Sew on buttons.

Be A Knit Whiz...

Bind off loosely

Make your bind-off row the same tension as the garment for the best knitting look.

Play hard and keep warm with this good-looking sweater...

The Side-Winder

A thick, cozy pullover with saddle shoulders and a slightly wider neck, which gives plenty of room for a shirt underneath. Or, as shown on the right on page 75, worn plain, with a soft yarn against your skin.

Yarn: Worsted Weight 12 (12-16-16) oz.
Blocked Measurement: 28 (30-32-34) inches for sweater at chest.
Gauge: In stockinette stitch (ss) 4½ stitches (sts) per inch.
Needles: Single point No. 5 and No. 8 or as needed to reach proper gauge. Double point No. 5
Cable needle.
Accessories: 2 st holders.

BACK

Cast on 62 (68-72-76) sts using smaller needles. Rib in k 1, p 1 for 1½ ins. Change to larger needles and continue in ss straight to 11 (11½-12-12) ins from bottom of ribbing. Check width: 14 (15-16-17) ins wide.

Armhole: Bind off 3 (3-4-4) sts beg of next 2 rows. Dec 1 st every other row at each armhole edge 2 (3-3-5) times. Continue straight to 4½ (5-6¼-6¾) ins from underarm.

Shoulder: Bind off 5 (6-6-6) sts beg of next 2 rows, 6 sts next 2 rows, and 6 (6-7-7) sts beg of next 2 rows. Place remaining 18 (20-20-20) sts on a holder.

FRONT

Same as back to 3½ (4-5¼-5¾) ins above underarm.

Start Neck: Place center 12 sts on a holder. Attach a 2nd ball of yarn so you can work both sides of neck at the same time. Dec 1 st at each neck edge every other row 3 (4-4-4) times. When armhole measures same as on back, bind off at each

shoulder edge 5 (6-6-6) sts 1 time, 6 sts 1 time and 6 (6-7-7) sts once.

SLEEVES (Make 2)

Cast on 30 (32-32-34) sts using smaller needles. Rib in k 1, p 1 for 2 ins, inc 6 (6-8-8) sts evenly across last row. Change to larger needles and continue in the following pattern, inc 1 st each end of needle every 1 (1¼-1½-1½) ins.:

Row 1:	K 10 (11-12-13), p 2, k 12, p 2, k 10 (11-12-13).
Row 2:	P 10 (11-12-13), k 2, p 12, k 2, p 10 (11-12-13).
Row 3:	K 10 (11-12-13), p 2, sl next 4 sts to dp needle and hold in back, k 4, k 4 from dp needle, k 4, p 2, k 10 (11-12-13).
Rows 4, 6, 8:	Same as row 2 adding any inc sts into ss areas as required.
Rows 5, 7:	Same as row 1 adding any inc into ss areas as required.
Row 9:	K 10 (11-12-13), p 2, k 4, sl next 4 sts to dp needle and hold in front, k 4, k 4 from dp needle, p 2, k 10 (11-12-13).
Rows 10, 12, 14:	Same as row 2, adding any inc as required.
Rows 11, 13:	Same as row 1, adding any inc as required.

Rep rows 3-14 until inc bring total sts to 52 (54-58-60). Continue straight to 13½ (15-17-17) ins from bottom of ribbing. Check width: 11 (11½-12-12½) ins wide at widest point.

Armhole: Bind off 4 sts beg of next 2 rows. Dec 1 st each end of needle every other row until 16 sts are left. Continue on these sts (the cable pattern) for an additional 4 ins. Bind off.

FINISHING

Sew side seams and sleeve seams. Insert sleeves into body and sew saddles.

Neckine: With right sides facing you and using smaller needles (dp), pick up approximately 74 (76-82-82) sts around neck. Rib in k 1, p 1 for 1 in. Bind off *loosely* in ribbing.

Block to size.

Wear it with everything, anytime, the whole year-round...

College Cable Pullover

**Your teenage boy or girl will love
wearing this popular sweater
as much as you'll enjoy knitting it.**

Yarn: Worsted Weight 12 (12-16-16) oz.
Blocked Measurement: 28 (30-32-34) inches for sweater at chest.
Gauge: In stockinette stitch (ss) 4½ stitches (sts) per inch, 6 rows per inch.
Needles: Single point No. 6 and No. 9 or as needed to reach proper gauge. Double point No. 6.
Accessories: St holders
Cable needle.

BACK OF SWEATER

Cast on 62 (68-72-76) sts using smaller needles. Rib in k 1, p 1 for 2 ins. Change to larger needles. Continue in ss straight to 12 ins from bottom of ribbing. Check width: 14 (15-16-17) ins wide.

Armhole: Bind off 2 sts beg of next 2 rows. Work 2 (2-4-2) rows even. Dec for full-fashion armhole as follows:
Row 1: K 2, sl 1, k 1, psso, k to last
   4 sts, k 2 tog, k 2.
Row 2: P across row.
Rep these 2 rows until 18 (20-20-20) sts remain. Place on holder.

FRONT OF SWEATER

Cast on 62 (68-72-76) sts using smaller needles. Rib in k 1, p 1 for 2 ins, inc 8 sts evenly across last row of ribbing. Change to larger needles. Continue in following pattern:

Row 1: K 14 (16-17-18), p 2, k 8, p 2, k 18
   (20-22-24), p 2, k 8, p 2, k 14
   (16-17-18).
Row 2: P 14 (16-17-18), k 2, p 8, k 2, p 18
   (20-22-24), k 2, p 8, k 2, p 14 (16-17-18).
Row 3: K 14 (16-17-18), p 2, sl next 4 sts to
   dp needle and hold in back, k 4 from dp
   needle (cable turn), p 2, k 18 (20-22-24),
   p 2, cable turn, p 2, k 14 (16-17-18).

Rows 4, 6, 8, 10, 12, 14: Same as row 2.
Rows 5, 7, 9, 11, 13: Same as row 1.
Rep rows 3-14 for cable pattern. When piece measures 12 ins from bottom of ribbing, start armholes. Check width: 14 (15-16-17) ins wide.

Armhole: Bind off 2 sts beg of next 2 rows. Then continue with dec for full-fashion armhole as on back. When 4½ (4½-5¼-5¾) ins above underarm, start neck: Place center 10 (12-10-12) sts on a holder (neck opening). Using 1 ball of yarn on each side of neck opening, work in pattern. Dec 1 st each side of neck opening every other row 5 times; at the same time contiue full-fashion armhole until 2 sts are left on each side. Bind off.

SLEEVES (Make 2)

Cast on 32 (32-32-36) sts using smaller needles. Rib in k 1, p 1 for 2 ins, inc 6 (6-8-8) sts evenly across last row of ribbing. Change to larger needles, following pattern and inc 1 st each end of needle every 1¼ ins:
Row 1: K 13 (13-14-16), p 2, k 8, p 2, k 13
   (13-14-16).
Row 2: P13 (13-14-16), k 2, p 8, k 2, p 13 (13-14-16).
Row 3: K 13 (13-14-16), p 2, cable turn, p 2,
   k 13 (13-14-16).
Rows 4, 6, 8, 10, 12, 14: Same as row 2 allowing inc in ss area.
Rows 5, 7, 9, 11, 13: Same as row 1 allowing inc in ss area.
Rep rows 3-14 allowing for required inc in ss area until there are 52 (54-58-60) sts on needle. Continue straight to 13½ (15-17-17) ins from bottom of ribbing. Check width: 10½ (11-11½-12) ins wide.

Armhole: Bind off 3 (2-2-2) sts beg of next 2 rows. Continue making full-fashion dec as on back until 4 sts remain. Bind off.

FINISHING

Sew in sleeves. Sew side and sleeve seam.

For Turtleneck: With right side facing, using smaller dp needles, pick up approximately 52 (60-62-62) sts around neck, including sts on holders. Rib in k 1, p 1 for 6 ins. Bind off *loosely* in ribbing.

A sweater to weather things in—beautifully...

The Mariner

Gorgeous Aran Isle stitches for your younger generation. This sweater (see page 74) is dressy or casual because it's covered with intricate knitting work. If you're a knitter who says a pattern that takes careful watching makes time go faster, this is for you.

Yarn: Worsted Weight 12 (12-12-16-16) oz.

Blocked Measurement: 26 (28-30-32-34) inches for sweater at chest.

Gauge: In stockinette stitch (ss) 4½ stitches (sts) per inch.

Needles: Straight No. 6 and No. 9 or as needed to reach proper gauge. Double point or cable needles.

Accessories: St holders.

Note: Be sure to practice the following design panels before starting the sweater:

DESIGN PANELS FOR MARINER SWEATER
Before you start knitting this sweater, practice each of the following six Aran patterns that will form the design. Also shown is the *Twist Rib* that will be used at the bottom of the back and front as well as on the cuffs of the sleeves.

Pattern A—Double Moss Stitch
Row 1:   (Wrong side): *K 1, p 1, rep from *.
Row 2:   Work sts *as you see them.*
Row 3:   *P 1, k 1, rep from *.
Row 4:   Work sts as you see them.
Rep rows 1 through 4.

Pattern B—Rope Stitch (2 sts)
Row 1:   (Wrong side): P 2.
Row 2:   K 2 tog but do not remove from needle, k the first of the 2 sts and sl both sts from the needle tog.
Rep above sequence.

Pattern C—Ladder (7 sts)
Row 1:   (Wrong side): P 7.
Rows 2, 4, 6: K 7.
Rows 3, 5, 7: P 7.
Row 8:   P 7.
Rep rows 1-8.

Pattern D—Ribbed Cable (7 sts)

Note: There are two "Row 2s" given. Each gives a different look to the cable. Practice both since you may prefer to use both in your garment.
Row 1:   (Wrong side): [P 1 through back of st (shown as p 1B), k 1] 3 times, p 1B.
Row 2:   Front Cross Cable (FCC): Sl first 3 sts to dp needle and hold in front, (k 1B, p 1) 2 times on next 4 sts, then from dp needle k 1B, p 1, k 1B.
Row 2:   Back Cross Cable (BCC): Sl next 4 sts to dp needle and hold in back, on next 3 sts k 1B, p 1, k 1B, then from dp needle (p 1, k 1B) 2 times.

Important: Although not stated in sweater patterns, you may prefer to do an FCC on one side of the center panel and a BCC on the other side; or if unsure of your knitting, select either version and use it throughout the garment.

Rows 3, 5, 7, 9: Same as Row 1.
Rows 4, 6, 8, 10: (K 1B, p 1) 3 times, k 1B.
Rep sequence of rows 1-10.

Pattern E—Trellis with Moss (28 sts)
Row 1:   (Wrong side): K 5, p 4, k 10, p 4, k 5.
Row 2:   P 5, sl next 2 sts to dp needle and hold in front, k 2B in next 2 sts, then from dp needle k 2B (called Front Double Cross or FDKC); p 10, FDKC, p 5.
Row 3 and all other wrong side rows: Work the sts as you see them.
Row 4:   P 4, sl next st to dp needle and hold in back, k 2B in next 2 sts, then p 1 from dp needle (called Back Cross or BC), sl next 2 sts to dp needle and hold in front, k next st, then k 2B from dp needle (called Front Cross or FC); p 8, BC, FC, p 4.
Row 6:   P 3, *BC, k 1, p 1, FC*, p 6, rep from * to *, p 3.
Row 8:   P 2, *BC, (k 1, p 1) 2 times, FC*, p 4,

72

rep from * to *, p 2.
Row 10: P 1, *BC, (k 1, p 1) 3 times, FC*, p 2, rep from * to *, p 1.
Row 12: *BC, (k 1, p 1) 4 times, FC, rep from *.
Row 14: *K 2B, (k 1, p 1) 5 times, FDKC, (k 1, p 1) 5 times, k 2B.
Row 16: *Sl 2 sts to dp needle and hold in front, *p next st,* then k 2B from dp needle (called Front Purl Cross or FPC); (k 1, p 1) 4 times, BC, rep from *.
Row 18: P 1, *FPC, (k 1, p 1) 3 times, BC*, p 2, rep from * to *, p 1.
Row 20: P 2, *FPC, (k 1, p 1) 2 times, BC*, p 4, rep from * to *, p 2.
Row 22: P 3, *FPC, k 1, p 1, BC*, p 6, rep from * to *, p 3.
Row 24: P 4, FPC, BC, p 8, FPC, BC, p 4.
Row 25: Same as row 3.
Rep rows 2-25 for pattern.

Pattern F—Half-Trellis with Moss (14 sts)
(In fronts of sweater, only).
Row 1: (Wrong side): K 5, p 4, k 5.
Row 2: P 5, FDKC, p 5.
Row 3: (And all other wrong side rows): Work sts as you see them.
Row 4: P 4, BC, FC, p 4.
Row 6: P 3, BC, k 1, p 1, FC, p 3.
Row 8: P 2, BC, (k 1, p 1) 2 times, FC, p 2.
Row 10: P 1, BC, (k 1, p 1) 3 times, FC, p 1.
Row 12: BC, (k 1, p 1) 4 times, FC.
Row 14: K 2B, (k 1, p 1) 5 times, k 2B.

Knit-Picking...

Going, growing, gone

For growing children, consider the raglan-sleeve style garment. It's one of the few sweater types that let's you knit with the child's growth in mind. The sweater won't sag at the shoulders, even when slightly bigger than the child's normal size.

Oops, a dropped stitch

To pick up a dropped stitch, work from the knit side (if possible). Use a crochet hook and pick up the strand lying behind the loop.

Row 16: FPC, (k 1, p 1) 4 times, BC.
Row 18: P 1, FPC, (k 1, p 1) 3 times, BC, p 1.
Row 20: P 2, FPC, (k 1, p 1) 2 times, BC, p 2.
Row 22: P 3, FPC, (k 1, p 1) BC, p 3.
Row 24: P 4, FPC, BC, p 4.
Row 25: Same as row 3.
Rep sequence of rows 2-25.

Twist Rib: This will be used in place of standard ribbing.
Row 1: *K 1B, p 1, rep from * across row.
Row 2: Rep row 1.
Rep these 2 rows as required in pattern.

BACK
Cast on 58 (62-68-72-76) sts using smaller needles. *Twist Rib* for 2½ ins inc 4 sts evenly across last row. Change to larger needles and establish aran design as follows:

Aran Design: Since each aran pattern has a different number of rows in its rep sequence, each will form its own panel. You will be able to follow the sequence of rows in each panel while working the entire back of the sweater. To start the design, work the next rows as shown:
Row 1: (Wrong side): *Pattern A* over next 6 (8-11-13-15) sts, *Pattern B,* k 1, *Pattern D,* k 1, *Pattern E,* k 1, *Pattern D,* k 1, *Pattern B, Pattern A* over last 6 (8-11-13-15) sts.
Row 2: *Pattern A* over first 6 (8-11-13-15) sts, *Pattern B,* p 1, *Pattern D,* p 1, *Pattern E,* p 1, *Pattern D,* p 1, *Pattern B, Pattern A* over last 6 (8-11-13-15) sts.

Continue in this fashion working each panel in accordance with its sequence of rows, working the st or sts separating the panels *as you see them:* K the k sts and p the p sts. When piece measures 11 (11½-12-12-12) ins from bottom of *Twist Rib,* start armhole. Blocked width: 13 (14-15-16-17) ins.

Armhole: Bind off 2 (3-3-4-4) sts beg of next 2 rows. Dec 1 st each armhole edge every other row 2 (2-3-3-5) times. Continue straight to 5½ (6-6½-7½-7¾) ins from underarm bind-off row.

Shoulder: Bind off 6 sts beg of next 4 rows; and 5 (6-7-8-8) sts beg of next 2 rows. Place balance of 20 (20-22-22-22) sts on holder.

FRONT
Same as back to 4 (4½-4½-5-5½) ins above underarm bind-off row. Place center 14 sts on holder for neckline. Using separate balls of yarn on each side of neck, dec 1 st at each neck edge every other row 3 (3-4-4-4) times. When armhole measures same as on back, bind off at each shoulder edge 6 sts 2

CONTINUED ON NEXT PAGE

CONTINUED FROM PREVIOUS PAGE
times and 5 (6-7-8-8) sts 1 time.

SLEEVES (Make 2)

Cast on 30 (30-32-32-34) sts using smaller needles. *Twist Rib* for 2 ins inc 6 sts evenly across last row. Change to larger needles and establish aran design as follows:

Row 1: (Wrong side): *Pattern A* over first 3 (3-4-4-5) sts, *Pattern D*, k 1, *Pattern F*, k 1, *Pattern D*, *Pattern A* over last 3 (3-4-4-5) sts.

Row 2: *Pattern A* 3 (3-4-4-5) sts, *Pattern D*, p 1, *Pattern F*, p 1, *Pattern D*, *Pattern A* 3 (3-4-4-5).

Continue working each panel in proper row sequence, working the sts separating the panels *as you see them*. Inc 1 st each end of needle every 1 in until there are 48 (52-54-56-58) sts, working all additional sts into the Double Moss Stitch (*Pattern A*). Continue straight until sleeve measures 12½ (13½-15-16-16½) ins from bottom of *Twist Rib*.

Armhole: Bind off 2 (2-3-3-5) sts beg of next 2 rows. Dec 1 st each end of needle every other row for 2½ (3-3½-4-4½) ins. Bind off 2 sts beg of next 4 rows. Bind off.

FINISHING

Sew shoulder seams.

Neckline: With right side facing you and using smaller needles, pick up approximately 56 (56-62-66-66) sts around neck. *Twist Rib* for 2 ins. Bind off *loosely* in ribbing pattern. Turn neck ribbing to inside of sweater so as to fold in half and tack in place.

Sew side and sleeve seams. Insert sleeves into armholes.

Tic Tac Toe (see next page)

The Side-Winder (see page 69)

Fun and games to make and the same to wear...

Tic Tac Toe

Set a happy mood for your favorite teen with the comfortable boat-neck pullover shown on the previous page. A fun, two-color sweater with tic tac toe embroidery is sure to be a hit!

Yarn: Worsted Weight 12 (12-16-16) oz. Small amount of contrasting colors.
Blocked Measurement: 28 (30-32-34) inches for sweater at chest.
Gauge: In stockinette stitch (ss) 4½ stitches (sts) per inch.
Needles: Single point No. 6 and No. 9.

BACK

Cast on 62 (68-72-76) sts with the smaller needle. Rib in k 1, p 1 for 2½ ins. Change to larger needles and continue in ss straight to 11½ (12-12-12) ins from the bottom of the ribbing. Blocked width of piece: 14 (15-16-17) ins.

Armhole: Bind off 3 (3-4-4) sts beg of next 2 rows. Dec 1 st every other row at each armhole edge 2 (3-3-5) times. Work straight to 4½ (5-6¼-6¾) ins from underarm. Change to a k 2, p 2 rib; and when the armhole measures 6 (6½-7¾-8¼) ins from bind-off, start the shoulders.

Shoulder: Bind off 6 sts beg of next 4 rows. Bind off balance 28 (32-34-34) sts.

FRONT

Same as the back.

SLEEVES (Make 2)

Cast on 28 (30-34-36) sts using smaller needles. Rib in k 1, p 1 for 2½ ins. Change to larger needles and inc 4 sts evenly across row. Work in ss and inc 1 st each end of needle every 1¼ ins to 48 (50-54-56) sts. Continue straight to 13½ (14½-15½-16½) ins from the bottom.

Armhole: Bind off 3 (3-4-4) sts beg of next 2 rows. Dec 1 st each end of needle every other row for 3 (3½-4-4½) ins. Bind off 2 sts beg of next 4 rows.

Bind off balance.

FINISHING

Sew shoulder seams, side seams and sleeve seams. Insert sleeves into armholes.

EMBROIDERY

Work the *Tic-Tac-Toe* design in either cross st or duplicate st as shown at right. Be sure to center the design across the body of the sweater. You can start the lines about 1 in above the ribbing.

(see instructions on page 19)

Be A Knit Whiz..

Right side up

When picking up an edge (see instructions on page 19) always work from the side *that will be seen.* Picked up stitches leave a slight ridge.

Don't knit in a vacuum

If something looks wrong, hot-foot it down to your yarn shop for help. All these patterns have been set up to be easy to read and error-free, but it's still possible something *could* go wrong.

Before you abandon your knitting in frustration, get some help to make sure you've done your knitting properly.

It's really worth the patience it takes to backtrack on a pattern to find a problem.

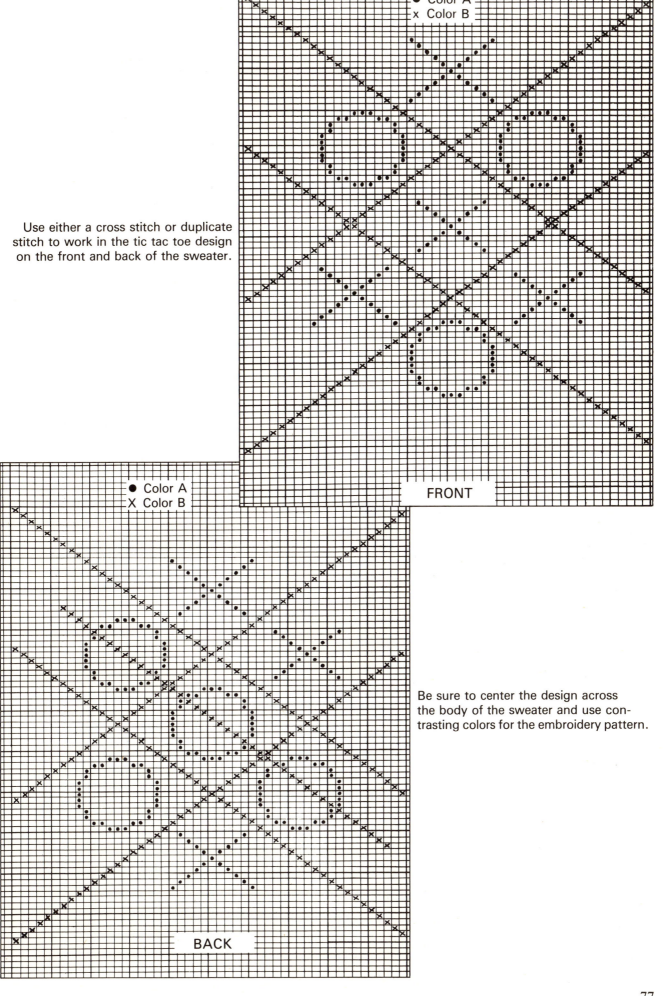

Use either a cross stitch or duplicate stitch to work in the tic tac toe design on the front and back of the sweater.

● Color A
x Color B

FRONT

● Color A
X Color B

Be sure to center the design across the body of the sweater and use contrasting colors for the embroidery pattern.

BACK

He'll love the pep of this sweater for years to come...

The Racer

**A comfortable crew neck dressed up with a subtle variegated yarn and a show-off stripe across the chest and arms.
It's perfect for school, casual dress or football in the park.**

Yarn: Worsted Weight 8 (12-12-16) oz. Main Color (MC). 1 (1-1-1) oz. Contrast Color (CC).
Blocked Measurement: 26 (28-30-32) inches for sweater at chest.

Gauge: In stockinette stitch (ss) 4½ stitches (sts) per inch.
Needles: Single point No. 6 and No. 9 or as needed to reach proper gauge. Double point No. 6.
Accessories: 2 st holders.

BACK

Cast on 58 (62-68-72) sts using smaller needles and MC. Rib in k 1, p 1 for 2½ ins. Change to larger needles and continue in ss straight to 10 (10½-11-12) ins from the bottom of the ribbing. Change to CC and work 4 rows in ss, then 2 rows in MC, and 2 rows in CC. Blocked width of piece: 13 (14-15-16) ins.

Armhole: With MC bind off 2 (3-3-4) sts beg of next 2 rows. Dec 1 st every other row at each armhole edge 2 (2-3-3) times. Work straight to 4½ (5-5½-6¼) ins. from the underarm.

Shoulder: Bind off 5 (5-6-7) sts beg of next 2 rows, 5 (6-6-7) sts beg of next 2 rows, and 6 sts beg of next 2 rows. Place the balance 18 (18-20-20) sts on a holder.

FRONT

Same as back to 4 (4½-4½-5¼) ins above the underarm. Place the center 12 sts on a holder. Attach a 2nd ball of yarn so you can work both sides of neck at the same time. Dec 1 st at each neck edge every other row 3 (3-4-4) times. When armhole measures same as back, bind off at each shoulder 5 (5-6-7) sts 1 time; 5 (6-6-7) sts 1 time; and 6 sts 1 time.

SLEEVES (Make 2)

Cast on 30 (30-32-32) sts with the smaller needles. Rib in k 1, p 1, for 2½ ins. Change to larger needles and inc 4 sts evenly across the row. Work in ss and inc 1 st at each end of needle every 1 in until 44 (48-50-54) sts. At the same time, when the sleeve measures 11 (12-13½-15) ins, work the color stripes as on the body of the sweater. Work straight to 12½ (13½-15-16½) ins from bottom of ribbing.

Armhole: Bind off 2 (3-3-4) sts beg of next 2 rows. Dec 1 st at each end of needle every other row for 2½ (3-3½-3½) ins. Bind off 2 sts beg of next 4 rows. Bind off balance.

FINISHING

Sew shoulder seams. With right side facing and dp needles, pick up approximately 52 (52-60-62) sts around neck. Rib in k 1, p 1 for 2 ins. Bind off loosely in ribbing. Turn half to inside and tack the neck down. Sew side seams and sleeve seams. Insert sleeves into body.

Be A Knit Whiz...

Get perfect set-in sleeves every time

To help you in knitting the set-in sleeve sweater patterns in this book, perhaps a word of explanation would help.

General sewing techniques were used when designing these sweaters. The sleeve caps are *deliberately* constructed 4-5 inches shorter than the armhole. But the top of the cap is almost 3 inches wide. *Stretch* the sleeve cap to fit into the armhole and you'll have a perfectly smooth armhole seam. And no puffy sleeves either!

Do you trust the label?

Most grosgrain ribbon you buy is marked "preshrunk." When you use it for your sweaters, it's a good idea to preshrink it *again*. Be safe, not sorry.

Got knitting tears in your eyes?

If you have to rip and reknit, SMILE...it only hurts for a little while. Any knitter who says she never rips and reknits, either doesn't care what her knitting looks like, or shades the truth!

Make it a Scot—a traditional sweater with solid, timeless appeal…

Highland Fling

So soft it's almost dressy. Warm and durable, it's just right for active kids. A really fantastic mosaic-striped yoke is this sweater's claim to fame.

Yarn: Worsted Weight 12 (12-16-16) oz Main Color (MC). 2 oz each of Colors A and B.

Blocked Measurement: 28 (30-32-34) inches for sweater at chest.

Gauge: In stockinette stitch (ss) 5 stitches (sts) per inch.

Needles: Single point No. 5 and No. 8 or as needed to reach proper gauge. Double point No. 5.

Accessories: 2 st holders.

PATTERN STITCH
Rows 1 and 2: Color A—k.
Row 3: Color B—k 1, *sl 1 with yarn held in back, k 1; rep from * across row.
Row 4: Color B—k 1, *sl 1 with yarn in front, k 1, rep from * across row.
Rows 5 and 6: Color A—k.
Row 7: Color B—k 2, *sl 1 with yarn in back, k 1; rep from * to last st, k 1.
Row 8: Color B—p 2, *sl 1 with yarn in front, p 1; rep from * to last st, p 1.
Row 9: Color B—k.
Row 10: Color B—p.
Row 11: MC—k.
Row 12: MC—p.

BACK
Cast on 70 (74-80-84) sts using the smaller needles. Rib in k 1, p 1 for 2½ ins, inc 1 st at the end of the last row. Change to larger needles and work in ss straight to 11½ (12-12-12) ins from the bottom of the ribbing. Blocked width of piece 14 (15-16-17) ins.

Armhole: Bind off 2 sts beg of next 2 rows. Work the next 2 rows even and at the same time start the pattern st here. Dec 1 st at each end of the needle every other row until 21 (23-23-23) sts remain. Place on a holder.

Note: Rep the 12 rows of the pattern st 3 times. Do not be concerned about the effect of the dec. It will not disturb the pattern.

FRONT
Same as the back to 4½ (4½-5½-5¾) ins above the underarm. Place the center 14 sts on a holder. Attach a 2nd ball of yarn so you can work both sides of the neck at the same time. Dec 1 st at each neck edge every other row 3 (4-4-4) times. Continue the raglan dec until 0 sts remain.

SLEEVES (Make 2)
Cast on 34 (34-36-38) sts using the smaller needles. Rib in k 1, p 1 for 2½ ins. Change to larger needles and inc 5 sts evenly across row. Work in ss and inc 1 st each end of needle every 1 in until 53 (57-61-63) sts. Continue straight to 13½ (14½-15½-16½) ins.

Armhole: Bind off 2 sts beg of next 2 rows. Work 0 (0-0-2) rows even and start the pattern st here as on the back. Dec 1 st every other row at each end of the needle until 1 st remains. Bind off.

FINISHING
Sew sleeves into body. Sew side and sleeve seams.

Neck: With right side facing you and dp needles, pick up approximately 62 (66-70-70) sts around the neck. Rib in k 1, p 1 for 2 ins. Bind off *loosely* in ribbing. Turn half of the neck ribbing to the inside and tack in place.

Left to right: **Pullover Set-in Sleeve Sweater** (page 66), **Winter Festival** (below), **College Cable Pullover** (page 71), and **Sweetheart Stripe** (page 84).

Swing into the sporting life...

Winter Festival

Show off your many-sided, fun-loving personality in the easy boat-neck sweater shown second from the left above. Four color panels are perfect for leftover yarn, and the sweater goes with everything!

Yarn: Worsted Weight 4 oz each of Colors A, B, C, D, E.
Blocked Measurement: 28 (30-32-34) inches for sweater at chest.
Gauge: In stockinette stitch (ss) 4½ stitches (sts) per inch.

Needles: Single point No. 7 and No. 9 or as needed to reach proper gauge.
Accessories: 3 bobbins for color E.
Note: In using colors, be sure to cross over the color strands so you won't leave a hole between the colors.

BACK
Cast on 64 (68-72-76) sts using smaller needle and color E. Work in ss and color pattern like this: 3 sts E, 27 (29-31-33) sts A, 4 sts E, 27 (29-31-33) sts B, 3 sts E. At 1 in k 1 row on the p side (hem row). Change to larger needles and continue in ss as before to 13 ins from the hem row.

Armhole: Bind off 3 (3-4-4) sts beg of next 2 rows. Dec 1 st every other row at each armhole edge 2 (3-3-5) times. Work straight to 6 (6½-7¾-8¼) ins from the underarm.

Shoulder: Bind off 6 sts beg of next 4 rows. On the remaining 30 (32-34-34) sts, work 1 in more, inc 1 st each end of the needle every row. Bind off loosely.

FRONT
Same as the back but substitute colors C and D for A and B.

SLEEVES (Make 2)
Cast on 32 (34-38-40) sts using the smaller needles and color D for one sleeve. (Use color B to cast on the second sleeve.) Work in ss 14 (15-17-18) sts color D, 4 sts E, 14 (15-17-18) sts Color A. At 1 in make a hem row, change to larger needles and continue in the established colors, inc 1 st each end of the needles every 1½ ins to 48 (50-54-56) sts. Continue straight to 13½ (14½-15½-16½) ins from the hem row.

Armhole: Bind off 3 (3-4-4) sts beg of next 2 rows. Dec 1 st each end of needle every other row for 3 (3½-4-4) ins. Bind off 2 sts beg of next 4 rows. Bind off balance.

For the second sleeve, after casting on with color B, set up color pattern: 14 (15-17-18) sts color B, 4 sts E, and 14 (15-17-18) sts color C. Continue as for first sleeve.

FINISHING
Assemble the sweater, matching up the colors of the body and sleeves. Sew shoulder seams, side and sleeve seams. Insert sleeves into the armholes. Turn the neck facing back to the wrong side and hem it in place. Turn up hems at the bottom and sleeve.

Be A Knit Whiz...

Crochet a pretty edge

This is one of the most commonly used edgings and, at the same time, one of the most difficult to do properly.

A garment should be assembled and blocked before the crocheted edge is added. The garment should have some draw-up on the finished edge—this means the finished crochet edge should be somewhat shorter than the edge you are working on. It will lay better. And, since the knitted edge is usually rippled, crocheting the edge will straighten it out, if applied properly.

Mark the midpoint of the edge (front bands, bottom of garment, etc.) with stainless steel T-pins. If the length is great, subdivide the edge a second and even third time. Now crochet it so the edge doesn't ruffle, but lays flat.

On neck edges, crocheting should not stand up like a mandarin collar. If it does, there are too many stitches.

Or, try this...

As an alternate to the crocheted front band, try 6-8 stitches more on each front at the center edge. Knit them in a knit 1, purl 1 rib along with the other stitches. The classic cardigans in this book were done this way. If you are changing a pattern to do this, be sure to take the additional stitches off when you reach the neckline.

Sweetheart Stripe

Cheerleading, riding a bike or dressing up for school will never be the same when your teen puts on the cheery striped pullover shown on page 82.

Yarn: Lightweight sport, Main Color (MC): 6 (6-8) oz; Stripe color A: 2 (2-2) 4 (4-6) oz; Stripe color B: 2 (2-2) 4 (4-6) oz.

Blocked Measurement: 32 (34-36) inches for sweater at chest.

Gauge: In stockinette stitch (ss) 5½ stitches (sts) per inch, 7½ rows per inch.

Needles: No. 3 and No. 5 or as needed to reach proper gauge. Double point No. 3.

Accessories: St holders.

BACK

Cast on 100 (104-110) sts using smaller sp needle. Rib in k 1, p 1 for 2 ins. Change to larger needles and continue in ss working striping pattern this way:

Row A:	6 rows color A	Row G:	2 rows B
Row B:	4 rows MC	Row H:	2 rows A
Row C:	4 rows color B	Row I:	4 rows MC
Row D:	2 rows MC	Row J:	2 rows B
Row E:	4 rows A	Row K:	4 rows MC
Row F:	8 rows MC		

Rep this striping pattern throughout sweater. When you are 12 ins from bottom of ribbing, start armhole.

Armhole: Bind off 2 sts beg of next 2 rows. Work 2 rows even. Dec 1 st every other row at each armhole edge until 28 (28-30) sts remain. Place on holder.

FRONT

Same as back to underarm. Divide the sts evenly. Using separate balls of yarn, work both sides at once working armhole edge as on back. Dec 1 st at each neck edge every 4 rows 14 (14-15) times, at same time continuing the raglan dec until 0 sts remain on each shoulder.

SLEEVES (Make 2)

Cast on 44 (46-48) sts using smaller sp needles. Rib in k 1, p 1 for 2½ ins. Change to larger needle inc 6 sts evenly across row. Work in color pattern like this:

Size 32: Start at row C—(See above). **Sizes 34-36:** Start at Row B—(See above). Working in color pattern as established, inc 1 st each end of needle every 1 in until 72 (74-74) sts. Continue straight to approximately 17 (18-18) ins from bottom of ribbing depending on matching of stripes.

Armhole: When determining point at which to start armhole on sleeves, be sure to choose the same row of color pattern for the sleeve underarm bind-off as on the underarm bind-off of the front and back. This may cause a slight variation in length of sleeve from that called for in the pattern. The color stripe matching is more important than the exact sleeve length.

Underarm:

Size 32 (34): Bind off 2 sts beg of next 2 rows. Work 2 (4) rows even. Dec 1 st each end of needle every other row until 2 sts remain. Bind off.

Size 36: Bind off 2 sts beg of next 2 rows. Dec 1 st each end of needle every 4th row 3 times, then every other row until 2 sts remain. Bind off.

FINISHING

Sew sleeves into body.

Neckline: With right side facing you and dp needles, pick up approximately 28 (28-30) sts across back of neck and 54 (56-59) sts on each front. Place ring marker on needle at V. Rib in k 1, p 1 until 2 sts before ring marker, k 2 tog, sl marker, sl 1, k 1 psso, complete round in k 1, p 1 rib. Rep for 1 in. Work a p row all around for a turn row. Now continue in ribbing but *inc* 1 st on each side of V marker every row until 1 in from turn row. Bind off *loosely* in ribbing. Turn neck to inside, using the p row as a turn row forming a hem edge. Tack down in place loosely. Sew side and sleeve seams. Block very lightly.

You'll love everything about this great look…

Sierra Tunic

Comfortable and practical…with lots of inventive stitch appeal. Our tunic (at the left on page 62) is perfect for active teens in jeans, slacks, blouses and turtlenecks… and a simple mosaic pattern too!

Yarn: Bulky 12 (16-20-24) oz Main Color (MC) and 2 (2-4-4) oz Contrast Color (CC).

Blocked Measurement: 28 (30-32-34) inches for tunic at bust.

Gauge: In stockinette stitch (ss) 3½ stitches (sts) per inch.

Needles: Single point No. 9 and No. 10½ or as needed to reach proper gauge.

Important: The color pattern is a mosaic technique—a simple way to handle colors. Just be sure you understand the technique before starting the tunic.

   1. On all right side rows, sl all sl sts as to p with the yarn held *behind* the needles.

   2. On all wrong side rows, sl all sl sts as to p with the yarn held in *front* of the needles.

   3. On all wrong side rows, k and sl the same sts that were knitted and slipped in the preceding right side row, using the same color yarn. So it's not necessary for us to give directions for the even numbered (wrong side) rows.

BACK

With MC cast on 48 (52-56-58) sts using smaller needle. Work in seed st (sds):

Row 1: K 1, p 1 across.

Row 2: P 1, k 1 across.

Rep these 2 rows for 8 rows more. Change to larger needles. Keeping the first 7 sts and the last 7 sts in seed st, work the balance of the sts in ss. Continue straight to 6 ins from the bottom of the band. At this point stop the seed st side borders and work the entire piece in ss to 9 ins from the bottom of the band. Start with the next k row: Using CC, k the next 2 rows. Start your color pattern here:

Row 1:   (Right side row) MC—k 1, *(sl 1, k 1) 2 times, sl 1, k 3; rep from * across the row.

Row 3:   (CC) k 1, *k 5, sl 1, k 3, sl 1; rep from * across.

Row 5:   (MC) k 1, *sl 1, k 1, sl 1, k 3, (sl 1, k 1) 2 times; rep from * across.

Row 7:   (CC) k 1, *k 3, (sl 1, k 1) 3 times, sl 1; rep from * across.

Row 9:   (MC) k 1, *sl 1, k 5, sl 1, k 3; rep from * across.

Row 11: (CC) k 1, *(k 1, sl 1) 3 times, k 4; rep from * across.

Row 13 and 14: MC—k both rows.

Row 15: Same as row 11.

Row 17: Same as row 9.

Row 19: Same as row 7.

Row 21: Same as row 5.

Row 23: Same as row 3.

Row 25: Same as row 1.

Rows 27 and 28: K both rows.

Work the next 4 rows in ss with the MC.

Armhole: Bind off 2 (2-3-3) sts beg of next 2 rows. Continue straight to 4½ (5-5¾-6¼) ins from the bind-off. Change to the smaller needles and work in k 1, p 1 ribbing for 6 rows.

Shoulder: Bind off 5 sts beg of next 2 rows, and 5 (6-7-7) sts beg of next 2 rows. Bind off balance—24 (26-26-28) sts.

FRONT

Same as back of tunic.

SLEEVES (Make 2)

With MC cast on 34 (36-40-44) sts using smaller needles. Work in seed st for 10 rows. Change to large needles and continue in ss inc 1 st each end of needle every 2½ ins 2 (3-3-3) times until 38 (42-46-50) sts. Work straight to 10 (11-12-13) ins or desired length.

Armhole: Bind off 2 (2-3-3) sts beg of next 2 rows. Dec 1 st each end of needle every other row 3 times. Bind off balance.

FINISHING

Sew shoulder seams. Sew side and sleeve seams. Insert sleeves into armholes.

Spread a little sunshine…

Fiesta Skirt

Here's the junior twin to our mother's Fiesta Skirt (see page 29) …just right for your little lady.

Yarn: Knitting Worsted Weight—2 skeins color A, 1 skein color B, 1 skein color C.
Sizes: (2-4) (6-8) (10-12).
Gauge: In stockinette stitch (ss) 4½ stitches (sts) per inch.
Needles: No. 9 circular needles or as needed to reach proper gauge.

SKIRT

With color A cast on 114 (130-142) sts. Join, being careful not to twist sts. Work in k 1, p 1 ribbing for 4 rows. Then *k 1, k 2 tog, yo; rep from * around. Change to color B and work 4 rows in k 1, p 1 ribbing. Inc 20 sts evenly around the needle.

**Change to color C and continue in all k st. Work color C for 1 in, 1 round color A, 2 rounds color C, 1 round color A, 2 ins color B.

3 rounds color A, 2 rounds color B, 1 round color A, 1 round color C.

1 round color A, 1 in color C, 1 round color A, 1 round color C, 1 round color B.

1 in color A, 3 rounds color B, 1 round color C, 2 ins color A. This is the 9 in length for size 2-4. If you wish to change length, add or subtract color pattern rows. At desired length, go to "bottom" of skirt section.

3 rounds color C, 2 rounds color B, 1 round color A.

1 round color C, 1 round color A, 1 in color B. This is the 11 in length for size 6-8. If you wish to change length, add or subtract color pattern rows. At desired length, go to "bottom" of skirt section.

1 round color A, 1 round color B, 1 round color C, 3 rounds color B, 1 in color A. This is the 13 in

length for size 10-12. For added length, rep colors from ** to desired length. Then go to "bottom" section.

Bottom: With color A, *k 1, k 2 tog, yo, rep from * across row. Work 2 rows in k 1, p 1. Bind off loosely.

FINISHING

Make a crochet cord (ch desired length and work 1 sc in each chain). Tassel both ends. Thread through holes in waistband and add wooden beads.

Tabard (see next page)

Let golden colors set the mood...

Tabard

It takes know-how to put a really sharp outfit together, but this great tunic (previous page) should make coordinating clothes a snap! A horizontal mosaic pattern trims the front and back—side and throat ties finish the look. Great for teens...but Mom likes it too!

Yarn: Knitting Worsted: 2, 4-oz skeins Main Color (MC), 1 skein each of three Contrasting Colors (CC) (black, brown, orange).

Sizes: 8/10, 12/14, 16/18.

Gauge: In stockinette stitch (ss) 4½ stitches (sts) per inch.

Needles: No. 9 or as needed to reach proper gauge.

Accessories: Size G or H crochet hook.

Important: Color Pattern Charts

1. When working odd numbered rows (right side rows): Sl the sl sts with the *yarn in back*.

2. When working even numbered rows (wrong side rows): Work sts same as the row before; that is, k the k sts and slip the sl sts BUT sl with the *yarn in front*. Because of this, we do not show instructions for the even numbered rows. *Simply follow the rule given above.*

3. Sizes are given as follows: Small (8/10) in front of parentheses, medium (12/14) in left half of parentheses, large (16/18) in right half of parentheses. Medium and large sizes are separated by a hyphen (-). An example would be as follows: k 1 (sl 1, k 3 - k 1). The medium size would be "sl 1, k 3", small and large sizes would be "k 1".

Chart A. Fretted Mosaic Pattern

Rows 1 and 2 (Orange): K across rows.

Row 3   (Brown): K 2 (5 - 2), * sl 1, k 5, rep from * to last 3 (0 - 3) sts. End sl 1 k 2 (0 - sl 1 k 2).

Row 5   (Orange): K 1 (sl 1 k 3 - k 1), * sl 1, k 1,

sl 1, k 3, rep from * to last 4 (1 - 4) sts. End sl 1 k 1 sl 1 k 1 (sl 1 - sl 1 k 1 sl 1 k 1).

Row 7   (Brown): K 0 (3 - 0), * sl 1, k 1, sl 1, k 3, rep from * to last 5 (2 - 5) sts. End sl 1 k 1 sl 1 k 2 (sl 1 k 1 - sl 1 k 1 sl 1 k 2).

Row 9   (Orange): K 1 (4 - 1), * sl 1, k 5, rep from * to last 4 (1 - 4) sts. End sl 1 k 3 (sl 1 - sl 1 k 3).

Row 10   (Orange): Complete 10th row following rule at top of page.

Chart B.   Assyrian Stripe Mosaic Pattern

Rows 1 and 2 (Brown): K across rows.

Row 3   (Black): K 1 (0 - 1), * sl 1, k 1, rep from * to last 0 (1 - 0) sts. End 0 (sl 1 - 0).

Row 5   (Brown): K 14 (1 - 4), * sl 1, k 15, rep from * to last 15 (2 - 5) sts. End sl 1 k 14 (sl 1 k 1 - sl 1 k 4).

Row 7   (Black): K 0 (k 3 - sl 1 k 1 sl 1 k 3), * sl 1, k 1, sl 1, k 1, sl 1, k 3, rep from * to last 5 (0 - 3) sts. End sl 1 k 1 sl 1 k 1 sl 1 (0 - sl 1 k 1 sl 1).

Row 9   (Brown): K 13 (0 - 3), * sl 3, k 13, rep from * to last 0 (3 - 6) sts. End 0 (sl 3 - sl 3 k 3).

Row 11   (Black): K 2 (5 - 0), * sl 1, k 7, rep from * to last 3 (6 - 1) sts. End sl 1 k 2 (sl 1 k 5 -sl 1).

Row 13   (Brown): K 1 (sl 3 k 1 - k 1 sl 1 k 1 sl 3 k 1), * sl 1, k 9, sl 1, k 1, sl 3, k 1, rep from * to last 12 (15-2) sts. End sl 1 k 9 sl 1 k 1 (sl 1 k 9 sl 1 k 1 sl 3-sl 1 k 1).

Row 15   (Black): K 2 (5 - 0), * sl 1, k 7, rep from * to last 3 (6 - 1) sts. End sl 1 k 2 (sl k 5 - sl 1).

Row 17   (Brown): K 13 (0 - 3), * sl 3, k 13, rep from * to last 0 (3 - 6) sts. End 0 (sl 3 - sl 3 k 3).

Row 19   (Black): K 0 (k 3 - sl 1 k 1 sl 1 k 3), * sl 1, k 1, sl 1, k 1, sl 1, k 3, rep from * to last 5 (0 - 3) sts. End sl 1 k 1 sl 1 k 1 sl 1 (0 - sl 1 k 1 sl 1).

Row 21   (Brown): K 14 (1 - 4), * sl 1, k 15, rep from * to last 15 (2 - 5) sts. End sl 1 k 14 (sl 1 k 1 - sl 1 k 4).

Row 23   (Black): K 1 (0 - 1), * sl 1, k 1, rep from * to last 0 (1 - 0) sts. End 0 (sl 1 - 0).

Rows 25 and 26 (Brown): K across row.

BACK

With MC cast on 77 (83-89) sts. Work in seed st for

12 rows. Next row (right side of knitting), work seed st over first 9 sts, k to last 9 sts, seed last 9 sts. Continue to work center sts in ss and side borders in seed until piece measures 3 ins from start. Work the next 6 rows in brown, 1 row black, 2 rows MC, 1 row black. Next 10 rows work Fretted Mosaic Pattern (chart A). Start pattern with orange. Next row after chart A, return to original pattern of ss and seed; work 1 row black, 2 rows MC, 1 row black. Work next 26 rows in Assyrian Stripe-Mosaic Pattern (chart B). Start with brown. Next row after chart B, return to original pattern with ss and seed; work 1 row black, 2 rows MC and 1 row black. Next 10 rows work chart A, then 1 black, 2 MC, 1 black, 6 brown. Continue in MC until piece measures 23 ins (23½-24) or desired length from the start.

SHOULDER
Bind off 6 (7-8) sts at the beg of next 6 rows and 7 sts beg of next 2 rows. Bind off balance 27 sts.

FRONT
Same as the back to 15 ins (15½-16) from the bottom. Work to the center st. Bind it off. Using two balls of yarn (one each side), continue up the front to 20 ins (20½-21) from the bottom.

NECK
At each neck edge, bind off 9 sts. Then dec 1 st at the same edge every other row 4 times. When the piece measures same as the back, bind off each shoulder 6 (7-8) sts 3 times, and 7 sts once.

FINISHING
Sew shoulders. Pull in all loose ends. With one of the colors, work 2 rows of sc around neck and front slit. Work 1 extra row of sc on neck. Put 2 sc ties at the neck front and make one or two sets of ties for the sides.

Be A Knit Whiz...

Pick what "seems" right for your seam

Basically, there are four types of seams:
Overcast, crocheted, woven and back-stitched.

Most people don't like the first two because they're bulky and give a "ropey" look to a finished seam.

If you knit evenly, maybe the woven seam is for you. But if you don't, the woven seams might turn out with a "mushy" look.

The back-stitched seam is the best all-round seam because of its great flexibility and strength. It's neat and inconspicuous. Woven seams are nice for attaching a front band or collar, or where a flat joint is required.

Here is how back-stitched and woven seams are made:

Backstitched Seam

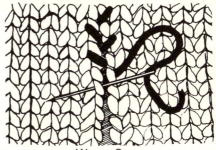
Woven Seam

Use the same yarn as in the garment when making a back-stitched seam, except:
1. When sewing a bulky sweater or jacket together.
2. When seaming a sweater made of mohair yarn.
3. When seaming a garment made with a boucle or textured yarn.
Then it's best to use a sportsweight or knitting worsted weight yarn.

Four Needle Mittens   Two Needle Mittens

Add a dash of color with zippy little stripes...

Basic Two and Four Needle Mittens

Just like our basic sweaters, you can knit all kinds of coloring and striped effects into these traditional mitten patterns. There's practically no difference between mittens knit on two or four needles—just a seam. But won't they look great with a favorite hat, scarf or winter coat?

90

Two Needle Mittens...
Yarn: Worsted Weight 2 (2-2) oz.
Sizes: Small (children), Medium (women), and Large (men).
Gauge: In stockinette stitch (ss) 5½ stitches (sts) per inch.
Needles: Single point No. 3 and No. 5.

MAKE TWO
Using smaller needles cast on 32 (44-48) sts. Rib in k 2, p 2 for 2½ ins. Change to larger needles and work in ss for 6 (6-8) rows.

SHAPE THUMB GUSSET
Row 1: K 15 (21-23) sts, put a marker on the needle, inc 1 st in each of the next 2 sts, k 15 (21-23) sts.
Row 2: And all even rows p.
Row 3: K to first marker, inc 1 st in next st, k to 1 st before 2nd marker, inc 1 st in next st. K to end of row. Rep rows 2 and 3 until there are 10 (12-14) sts between the markers, ending with a p row. On the next row k to first marker sl these 15 (21-23) sts to a holder, k to next marker, turn and put the remaining 15 (21-23) sts on another holder.

THUMB
Working on 10 (12-14) sts, cast on 1 st at the beg of each of the next 2 rows. Work even in ss on 12 (14-16) sts until piece measures desired length, ending with a p row. K 2 tog across the row. Break off yarn leaving a 12 in end. Draw yarn through all the sts on the needles and pull up tight. Fasten off the end.

HAND
Sl 15 (21-23) sts onto needles, join yarn at the base of the thumb and pick up 2 sts over thumb, then work the sts from the other holder onto the same needles. Work even in ss on 32 (44-48) sts, until piece measures 1½ ins less than desired finished length. End with a p row.
Next Row: *K 2 tog, k 4 rep from * across row.
Row 2: P.
Row 3: *K 2 tog, k 3 rep from * across. Continue in this manner to dec every other row until there are 6 sts remaining. Break off yarn leaving a 10 in length. Finish this tip the same as the thumb.

Four Needle Mittens...
Yarn: Worsted Weight 2 (2-2) oz.
Sizes: Small (children), Medium (women), and Large (men).
Gauge: In stockinette stitch (ss) 5½ stitches (sts) per inch.
Needles: Double point No. 3 and No. 5.

MAKE TWO
Using smaller needles cast on 36 (42-48) sts. Divide on 3 needles and join being careful not to twist sts. K 1, p 1 in ribbing for 2½ ins. Change to larger needles and k round and round for 6 (6-8) rows.

THUMB
Round 1: Starting at the beg of a round k 4, put a marker on the needle, inc 1 st in each of the next 2 sts, put a marker on needle, k to end of round.
Round 2: And all even rounds: K.
Round 3: K to first marker, inc 1 st in next st, k to 1 st before next marker, inc 1 st in next st, k to end of round. Rep rounds 2 and 3 until there are 10 (12-14) sts between the markers, end with round 2.
Next Round: K to first marker, sl next 10 (12-14) sts to a holder to be worked later for thumb. Cast on 2 sts over this opening, k to the end of round. Continue to k round and round on 36 (42-48) sts until piece measures 1½ ins less than desired finished length.
Next Round: *K 2 tog, k 4 (5-6), rep from * to end of round.
Round 2: And all even rounds: K.
Round 3: *K 2 tog, k 3 (4-5) sts, rep from * to end of round. Continue in this manner to dec 6 sts every round, having 1 st less between dec until 6 sts remain. Break off yarn, leaving a 10 in length. Draw yarn through sts and pull up tightly. Fasten off.

THUMB
Sl 10 (12-14) sts from holder onto larger needles and join yarn, picking up sts over cast on sts. Continue in ss, dec 1 st at each corner on next round until piece measures desired length. Break off yarn leaving a 12 in length. Finish in same manner as tip of mitten.

You won't be able to resist these two little show-off pillows…

Toss Pillows

**Two mosaic-patterned pillows with
designs so bright they
almost jump up off the knitting!
(No. 1 lower right, No. 2 upper
left on page 94). Make them
a cheery color to coordinate
your decorating scheme.**

Yarn: Worsted Weight, for each pillow
4 oz Color A, 4 oz Color B.
Needles: Single point No. 10.
Accessories: Aluminum or plastic size I
crochet hook.
Important: The color pattern is a
mosaic technique—a simple way to handle colors. Just be sure you understand
the technique before starting the pillows.

1. On all right side rows, sl all sl sts as to p with the
yarn held *behind* the needles.

2. On all wrong side rows, sl all sl sts as to p with
the yarn held in *front* of the needles.

3. On all wrong side rows, k and sl the same sts
that were knitted and slipped in the preceding right
side row, using the same color yarn. So it's not
necessary for us to give directions for the even
numbered (wrong side) rows.

TOSS PILLOW NO. 1
Cast on 56 sts with color A and k one row.
Row 1:   (Right side)—with B, k 1, *(sl 1, k 1)
10 times, sl 1, k 3, sl 1, k 1, sl 1, k 23,
(sl 1, k 1) twice; end k 1.
Row 2:   And all other wrong-side rows—p or k
the same sts worked on the previous row,
with the same color yarn; and sl all the
same sl sts with the yarn in *front*.

Note: On our models, the wrong side rows were p.
Experiment to see which you prefer.

Row 3:   With A—k 1, *k 7, k 1, k 13, sl 1, k 3,
sl 1, k 1; rep from *, end k 1.
Row 5:   With B—k 1, *(sl 1, k 1) twice, sl 1,
k 5, (sl 1, k 1) 4 times, (sl 1, k 3) twice,
sl 1; rep from *, end k 1.
Row 7:   With A—k 1, *k 5, sl 1, k 3, sl 1, k 9,
(sl 1, k 3) twice; rep from *, end k 1.
Row 9:   With B—k 1, *(sl 1, k 1, sl 1, k 3) twice,
(sl 1, k 1) twice, (sl 1, k 3) twice, sl 1, k 1,
sl 1; rep from *, end k 1.
Row 11: With A—k 1, *k 3, sl 1, k 7, sl 1, k 5,
sl 1, k 3, sl 1, k 5; rep from *, end k 1.
Row 13: With B—k 1, *sl 1, k 3, (sl 1, k 1) 3 times,
(sl 1, k 3) 3 times, (sl 1, k 1) twice, sl 1;
rep from *, end k 1.
Row 15: With A—k 1, *k 3, sl 1, k 7, (sl 1, k 3)
twice, sl 1, k 7; rep from *, end k 1.
Row 17: With B—k 1, *(sl 1, k 1, k 3) twice,
(sl 1, k 3) twice, (sl 1, k 1) 3 times, sl 1;
rep from *, end k 1.
Row 19: With A—k 1, *k 5, (sl 1, k 3) 3 times,
sl 1, k 9; rep from *, end k 1.
Row 21: With B—k 1, *(sl 1, k 1) twice, sl 1, k 5,
(sl 1, k 3) twice, (sl 1, k 1) 4 times, sl 1;
rep from *, end k 1.
Row 23: With A—k 1, *k 7, (sl 1, k 3) 3 times,
sl 1, k 7; rep from *, end k 1.
Row 25: With B—k 1, *(sl 1, k 1) 4 times, (sl 1,
k 3) twice, sl 1, k 5, (sl 1, k 1) twice,
sl 1; rep from *, end k 1.
Row 27: With A—k 1, *k 9, (sl 1, k 3) 3 times,
sl 1, k 5; rep from *, end k 1.
Row 29: With B—k 1, *(sl 1, k 1) 3 times, (sl 1,
k 3) 3 times, sl 1, k 1, sl 1, k 3, sl 1, k 1,
sl 1; rep from *, end k 1.
Row 31: With A—k 1, *k 7, (sl 1, k 3) twice, sl 1,
k 7, sl 1, k 3; rep from *, end k 1.
Row 33: With B—k 1, *(sl 1, k 1) twice, (sl 1,
k 3) 3 times, (sl 1, k 1) 3 times, sl 1, k 3,
sl 1; rep from *, end k 1.
Row 35: With A—k 1, *k 5, sl 1, k 3, sl 1, k 5,
sl 1, k 7, sl 1, k 3; rep from *, end k 1.
Row 37: With B—k 1, *sl 1, k 1, (sl 1, k 3) twice,
(sl 1, k 1) twice, sl 1, (k 3, sl 1, k 1, sl 1)
twice; rep from *, end k 1.
Row 39: With A—k 1, *(k 3, sl 1) twice, k 9, sl 1,
k 3, sl 1, k 5; rep from *, end k 1.
Row 41: With B—k 1, *(sl 1, k 3) twice, (sl 1,

k 1) 4 times, sl 1, k 5, (sl 1, k 1) twice, sl 1; rep from *, end k 1.

Row 43: With A—k 1, *k 1, sl 1, k 3, sl 1, k 13, sl 1, k 7; rep from *, end k 1.

Row 45: With B—k 1, *sl 1, k 1, sl 1, k 3, (sl 1, k 1) 10 times; rep from *, end k 1.

Row 47: With A—k 1, *(k 1, sl 1) twice, k 23; rep from *, end k 1.

Row 49: With B—k 1, *k 23, (sl 1, k 1) twice, rep from *, end k 1.

Row 50: See row 2.

Rows 51-100: Rep rows 1-50, reversing colors: Color A for the first 2 rows; color B for the next 2 rows, etc.

Make two pieces the same: One for the back and one for the front. Using the I crochet hook and either one of the colors, join the two pieces—wrong side to wrong side. Work one row of sc on 3 sides, being sure your hook goes through both pillow faces. Do not break off yarn. Insert your pillow form or stuffing and then close up the 4th side, continuing the sc edge. Fasten off.

TOSS PILLOW NO. 2

Cast on 57 sts with Color A and p 1 row.

Row 1: (Right side)—with color B—k 2, *sl 1, k 2, (sl 1, k 4) twice, sl 1, k 2, sl 1, k 1; rep from *, end k 1.

Row 2: And all other wrong side rows: P (or k) the same sts worked on the previous row using the same color; and sl all the same sl-sts with the yarn in *front*.

Row 3: With A—k 1, *sl 1, k 4, sl 1, k 1, sl 1, k 3, sl 1, k 1, sl 1, k 4; rep from *, end sl 1, k 1.

Row 5: With B—k 3, *sl 1, k 5, sl 1, k 1, sl 1, k 5, sl 1, k 3; rep from *.

Row 7: With A—k 2, *(sl 1, k 1) twice, sl 1, k 7, (sl 1, k 1) 3 times; rep from *, end k 1.

Row 9: With B—k 7, *(sl 1, k 1) 3 times, sl 1, k 11; rep from *, end last rep k 7.

Row 11: With A—k 2, *sl 1, k 1, (sl 1, k 5) twice, (sl 1, k 1) twice; rep from *, end k 1.

Row 13: With B—k 5, *sl 2, k 7; rep from *, end last rep k 5.

Row 15: With A—k 1, *sl 1, k 5, (sl 1, k 1) 3 times, sl 1, k 5; rep from *, end sl 1, k 1.

Row 17: With B—k 2, *sl 1, k 1, sl 1, k 11, (sl 1, k 1) twice; rep from *, end k 1.

Row 19: With A—k 5, *(sl 1, k 1) 5 times, sl 1, k 7; rep from *, end last rep k 5.

Row 21: With B—k 2, *sl 1, k 5, sl 1, k 3, sl 1, k 5, sl 1, k 1; rep from *, end k 1.

Row 23: With A—k 3, *sl 1, k 1, (sl 1, k 4) twice, sl 1, k 1, sl 1, k 3; rep from *.

Row 25: With B—k 1, *sl 1, k 4, sl 1, k 2, sl 1, k 1, sl 1, k 2, sl 1, k 4; rep from *, end sl 1, k 1.

Row 27: With A, k.

Row 28: With A—p (or k).

Rep these 28 rows until your pillow is the desired size.

Make two pieces the same: One for the back and one for the front. Using the I crochet hook and either one of the colors, join the two pieces—wrong side to wrong side. Work one row of sc on 3 sides, being sure your hook goes through both pillow faces. Do not break off yarn. Insert your pillow form or stuffing and then close up the 4th side, continuing the sc edge. Fasten off.

Knit-Picking...

Always clean, always new

Wool should always be washed in pure soaps, not detergent.

Detergents can strip the natural oils from wool, and even make colored yarns bleed! Before you know it, all your beautiful knitting looks matted and old.

Use lukewarm water with soap, and then rinse. In the final rinse, add a teaspoon of soap to give softness and fluffiness. Roll your knitted garment in a towel to remove excess water.

Never pick up a wet knit sweater by the sleeves or shoulders. Scoop it up and spread out flat on a drying surface.

Follow the yarn manufacturer's instructions for care of any of your garments made from synthetics.

Brave the cold in style…

Striped Stocking Cap/Scarf Set

Here's a super-stretchy pair that you can easily pull on for a snugger fit when it's really cold outside. It's cute in any three-color combination, and perfect for all ages.

Yarn: Worsted Weight, 4 oz each in Colors A and B, 2 oz in Color C.
Needles: For hat, single point No. 6 and No. 8. For scarf, single point No. 10½.

Color Pattern
Rows 1 and 3: K Color A.
Rows 2 and 4: P Color A.
Rows 5 and 6: K Color B.
Row 7: Color C—k 1, * sl 1 with yarn in back, k 1; rep from * across.
Row 8: Color C—k 1, *sl 1 with yarn in front, k 1; rep from * across.
Rows 9 and 10: K Color B.
Row 11: Color A—k 2, sl 1 with yarn in back, k 1; rep from * across end k 1.
Row 12: Color A—p 2, *sl 1 with yarn in front, p 1; rep from * across end p 1.
Rep these 12 rows for the length of the scarf and hat.

SCARF
Cast on 35 sts with No. 10½ needle. Work in striping pattern for 48 ins or desired length. Bind off loosely. Work 1 row sc on each end and then fringe with the 3 colors.

HAT
With Color B, cast on 89 sts using No. 6 needles. Rib in k 1, p 1 for 5 ins. Change to No. 8 needles and continue in the color pattern for 3 ins. Dec 10 sts evenly across. Continue with the color striping and rep the dec row every 1½ ins until 49 sts remain. Work straight until piece measures 13½ ins from the top of the ribbing. Break off yarn leaving a long thread. Thread through a yarn darner and run it through all sts on the needles. Pull sts up tightly and fasten off the top. Sew up the back of the hat and attach a tassel to the end.

Let the wind blow—this easy set is as warm as toast...

English Rib Hat and Scarf Set

A thick, ribbed cap and scarf for adults and children alike in an easy-to-follow technique. Bulky yarn and jiffy pom-poms maximize the sporty look.

Yarn: Bulky 14 oz.
Needles: Single Point No. 9 and No. 10.

Pattern Stitch:
Row 1: P.
Row 2: *P l, k l st in row below; rep from * to last st, k l. Rep row 2 for the entire pattern.

HAT

Cast on 36 sts using No. 10 needle. Work in patern st for 5 ins. Change to No. 9 and continue in p l, k l rib for 2 ins. K 2 tog across the needle. Break yarn leaving a long end. Thread a tapestry needle and slide it through all of the sts on the needle. Draw the sts up tightly and weave the back seam tog. Make a pom-pom and attach it to the top of the hat.

SCARF

With No. 10 needle, cast on 24 sts. Work in pattern st for 60 ins or desired length. Break off yarn leaving a long thread. As for the hat, thread a needle and slip all the sts off onto the yarn. Draw up and fasten off. Make a pom-pom for each end.

Chevron Hat and Scarf Set

A chic little hat and scarf set that's sure to brighten up gloomy fall and winter days. Tiny chevron designs, tasseled ends on the scarf and a turned up edge on the hat are sure to be popular with everyone.

Yarn: Worsted Weight 12 oz.
Needles: No. 3, No. 6 and No. 10½.

SCARF

Cast on 33 sts using No. 10½ needles. Work in pattern st as follows:

Row 1: *K 1, p 1, k 1, p 1, k 5, p 1; rep from * 2 more times; end k 1, p 1, k 1.
Row 2: *P 3, k 2, p 3, k 2; rep from *2 times more; end p 3.
Row 3: *K 1, p 1, k 1, p 3, k 1, p 3; rep from * 2 times more; end k 1, p 1, k 1.
Row 4: *P 3, k 7; rep from *2 times more; end p 3.
Row 5: *K 1, p 1, k 2, p 5, k 1; rep from * 2 times more; end k 1, p 1, k 1.
Row 6: P 5, *k 3, p 2; rep from * 5 times more; end p 3.
Row 7: *K 1, p 1, k 4, p 1, k 3; rep from * 2 times more; end k 1, p 1, k 1.
Row 8: P across the row.

Rep these 8 rows until piece measures 60 ins. Bind off loosely. Block. Fringe the narrow ends.

CAP

Cast on 92 sts using No. 3 needles. Rib in k 1, p 1 for 1¼ ins. Inc 1 st at the end of the last row. Change to No. 6 needles and work in pattern st for 3½ ins.

First Dec Row: *K 2 tog, k 1; rep from * across the row. Continue in ss for 1½ ins. Rep the dec row and work another 4 rows in ss. Break off yarn leaving an 18 in length. Thread the yarn through a darning needle and run the needle through all the sts on the knitting needles. Draw the sts up tightly and fasten well. Sew the back seam with a weaving seam. Attach a tassel, crocheted loop or a button to the top of the hat.

Snuggle up by the fire—with this beautiful, knitted...

Aran Afghan or Car Robe

A thick, seven-panel afghan rich with the detail of four story-telling designs. The pattern is interesting in whatever colors you choose and perfect for yourself or as a gift.

Yarn: Bulky, or Knitting Worsted Weight with double strand. 8 pink, 8 red, 8 white, 3 blue in bulky 2-oz skeins or 4 pink, 4 red, 4 white, 2 blue in knitting worsted 4-oz skeins.

Approximate finished size: Afghan 47 by 56 inches. Car Robe 35 by 56 inches.

Gauge: In stockinette stitch (ss) 3½ stitches (sts) per inch.

Needles: Single point No. 10½ or as needed to reach proper gauge. Double point needles for cables.

Note: This afghan is made of seven panels, each 56 inches long. You need to make 2 each of panels A, B, and C. Make 1 of panel D for the center.

Panel 1—Red Yarn
Horse-shoe Cable (28 st) (Make 2)
Cast on 28 sts and p 1 row. Start pattern as follows:
Row 1: K 2, p 2, k 20, p 2, k 2.
Row 2: All even rows: K 4, p 20, k 4.
Rows 3, 5, and 7: Same as row 1.
Row 9: K 2, p 2, sl next 5 sts to cable needle and hold in back, k next 5 sts, k 5 from cable needle, sl next 5 sts to cable needle and hold in front, k next 5 sts, k 5 from cable needle, p 2, k 2.
Rows 10, 12, and 14: Same as row 2.
Rows 11 and 13: Same as row 1.
Rep above 14 rows to desired length (afghan or car robe). Bind off in pattern.

Panel 2—Pink Yarn
Mountain Trail (26 st) (Make 2)
Cast on 26 sts and p 1 row. Start pattern as follows:
Row 1: K 2, p 1, k 2 tog, but do not drop from left needle, k the first st and remove both

from needle (rope st), p 1, k 11, p 1, k 1; p 2, rope st, p 1, k 2.
Row 2: K 3, p 2, k 1, p 1, k 1, p 1, k 1, p 10, k 1, p 2, k 3.
Row 3: K 2, p 1, rope st, p 1, k 9, p 1, k 1, p 1, k 2, p 1, rope st, p 1, k 2.
Row 4: K 3, p 2, k 1, p 3, k 1, p 1, k 1, p 8, k 1, p 2, k 3.
Row 5: K 2, p 1, rope st, p 1, k 7, p 1, k 1 p 1, k 4, p 1, rope st, p 1, k 2.
Row 6: K 3, p 2, k 1, p 5, k 1, p 1, k 1, p 6, k 1, p 2, k 3.
Row 7: K 2, p 1, rope st, p 1, k 5, p 1, k 1, p 1, k 6, p 1, rope st, p 1, k 2.
Row 8: K 3, p 2, k 1, p 7, k 1, p 1, k 1, p 4, k 1, p 2, k 3.
Row 9: K 2, p 1, rope st, p 1, k 3, p 1, k 1, p 1, k 8, p 1, rope st, p 1, k 2.
Row 10: K 3, p 2, k 1, p 9, k 1, p 1, k 1, p 2, k 1, p 2, k 3.
Row 11: K 2, p 1, rope st, p 1, k 1, p 1, k 1, p 1, k 10, p 1, rope st, p 1, k 2.
Row 12: K 3, p 2, k 1, p 11, k 1, p 1, k 2, p 2, k 3.
Row 13: Same as row 11.
Row 14: Same as row 10.
Row 15: Same as row 9.
Row 16: Same as row 8.
Row 17: Same as row 7.
Row 18: Same as row 6.
Row 19: Same as row 5.
Row 20: Same as row 4.
Row 21: Same as row 3.
Row 22: Same as row 2.
Rep rows 1-22 for pattern until panel is desired length. Bind off in pattern.

Panel 3—White Yarn
Tree of Life (21 st) (Make 2)
These abbreviations are used: WYIF = with yarn in front; WYIB = with yarn in back.
Cast on 21 sts and p 1 row. Start pattern as follows:
Row 1: K 3, p 2, k 1, p 4, sl 1 WYIB, p 4, k 1, p 2, k 3.
Row 2: K 2, p 1, k 2, sl 1 WYIF, k 4, p 1, k 4, sl 1 WYIF, k 2, p 1, k 2.
Row 3: K 3, p 2, (sl 1 st to dp needle and hold in front, p 1, k 1 from dp needle) (FC), p 3, sl 1 WYIB, p 3, (sl 1 to dp needle and hold in back, k 1, p 1 from dp needle)

CONTINUED ON NEXT PAGE

(BC), p 2, k 3.

Row 4: K 2, p 1, k 3, sl 1 WYIF, k 3, p 1, k 3, sl 1 WYIF, k 3, p 1, k 2.
Row 5: K 3, p 3, FC, p 2, sl 1 WYIB, p 2, BC, p 3, k 3.
Row 6: K 2, p 1, k 4, sl 1 WYIF, k 2, p 1, k 2, sl 1 WYIF, k 4, p 1, k 2.
Row 7: K 3, p 4, FC, p 1, sl 1 WYIB, p 1, BC, p 4, k 3.
Row 8: K 2, p 1, k 5, sl 1 WYIF, k 1, p 1, k 1, sl 1 WYIF, k 5, p 1, k 2.
Row 9: K 3, p 2, k 1, p 2, FC, sl 1 WYIB, BC, p 2, k 1, p 2, k 3.
Row 10: K 2, p 1, k 2, sl 1, WYIF, k 4, p 1, k 4, sl 1 WYIF, k 2, p 1, k 2.

Rep rows 3-10 to desired length. Bind off in pattern.

Panel 4—Blue Yarn
Diamond in the Rough (19 st) (Make 1)
Cast on 19 sts. Continue in pattern as follows:
Row 1: K 2, p 1, k 5, p 1, k 1, p 1, k 5, p 1 k 2...wrong side.
Row 2: K 3, p 5, sl next 2 sts to dp needle and hold in front, k 1 through back of st (k 1b), sl the p st from dp needle to left hand needle and p it, then k 1b from dp needle, p 5, k 3.
Row 3: Same as row 1.
Row 4: K 3, p 4, sl next st to dp needle and

hold in back, k 1b, then p 1 from dp needle (BC), k 1, sl next st to dp needle and hold in front, p 1, then k 1b from dp needle (FC), p 4, k 3.
Row 5: And all odd rows, k 2, p 1, work next 13 sts as you see them, p 1, k 2.
Row 6: K 3, p 3, BC, k 1, p 1, k 1, FC, p 3, k 3.
Row 8: K 3, p 2, BC, (k 1, p 1) 2 times, k 1, FC, p 2, k 3.
Row 10: K 3, p 1, BC, (k 1, p 1) 3 times, k 1, FC, p 1, k 3.
Row 12: K 3, BC, (k 1, p 1) 4 times, k 1, FC, k 3.
Row 14: K 3, FC, (p 1, k 1) 4 times, p 1, BC, k 3.
Row 16: K 3, p 1, FC, (p 1, k 1) 3 times, p 1, BC, p 1, k 3.
Row 18: K 3, p 2, FC, (p 1, k 1) 2 times, p 1, BC, p 2, k 3.
Row 20: K 3, p 3, FC, (p 1, k 1), p 1, BC, p 3, k 3.
Row 22: K 3, p 4, FC, p 1, BC, p 4, k 3.

Rep rows 1-22 to desired length. Bind off in pattern.

FINISHING AFGHAN or ROBE

Sew or crochet panels together.

Use yarn of same color as Panel 3 for fringe (Yarn requirements were computed on this basis. If you use another color you probably will need additional yarn). At corner of each panel place a fringe of same color as panel. Cut fringe to length of 6 or 7 ins, using double strand of bulky or 4 strands of knitting worsted.

Be A Knit Whiz...

Get ready, set—measure!

It's always a good idea to measure your knitting as you go along, no matter how expert you are.

Why? Because you can go off gauge if you're tired or distracted...or if a certain television spy movie has you momentarily *spellbound.*

Measure each piece of the garment from time to time to recheck the gauge. Measure the entire width. If the piece is within a half inch of the required measurement, all is well. If you find you've got a 24 inch piece when you should have a 22 or 26 inch wide piece, you've got trouble. Rip back to where you were last on size and re-knit. Maybe you need to change the size of your needle.

To measure, use a smooth hard surface and a hard ruler or yardstick. Do NOT use a tape measure—it won't work. Carefully slide enough stitches off the needle so the piece can be flattened out evenly throughout the width *without stretching any portion.* (Be careful not to pull out the stitches so you can ease them back into the needle when you're through measuring.) Be sure to measure lengths of pieces too.

Think warm—it's cold outside...

Winter Helmet

This simple pull-on hat can be worn over the nose and mouth, or with most of your face showing. Tucked inside a coat, its long neck flaps keep the wind off the chest and ears. This helmet is a perfect topper for walking in the woods, delivering papers or going to school. Knit in children's and adult sizes.

Yarn: Knitting Worsted Weight, two, 4-oz skeins.
Gauge: In stockinette stitch (ss) 5½ stitches (sts) per inch.
Needles: Single point No. 6 and No. 8.
Note: Use the numbers in parentheses for children's sizes.

FRONT

With No. 8, cast on 60 (50) sts. K 5 (3) in in garter st. Next row dec 12 sts by k every 4th and 5th (3rd and 4th) tog until 48 (38) sts left. With No. 6, work in ribbing k 2, p 2 for 6 (3) in. Change back to No. 8. Next row start face opening as follows: Work 10 (7) sts, sl these sts on holder, bind off 28 (24) sts, on remaining 10 (7) sts continue ribbing for 12 (8) rows, break yarn. Work across 10 (7) sts on holder and work 11 (7) rows more. Then cast on 28 (24) sts over the bound off sts and join to the 10 (7) sts at other side—48 (38) sts on needles. Continue ribbing for 4 (3) in; then dec for top of helmet as follows:

Row 1: K 2, k 2 tog, k 14 (10),
k 2 tog, k 14 (10), k 2 tog, k 12 (10).
Row 2: P.
Row 3: K 2, k 2 tog, k 13 (9), k 2 tog, k 13 (9),
k 2 tog, k 11 (8).
Row 4: P.

Continue to dec 3 sts every k row (having 1 st less between dec) until top piece measures 2 ins, or 9 sts remain. Put on holder. Leave a long thread and pull thru sts on holder and draw up tight. Fasten off.

BACK

Work same as front, omitting face opening.

FINISHING

Join back and front, starting seam at start of ribbing.

Toast your tootsies by the fire…

Knitted Lace-up Slippers

Let yourself go with the wildest colors you can find! These warm pull-on slippers are popular with everyone from college students to grandpa relaxing in his favorite reading chair.

Yarn: Worsted Weight 2 oz Color A, 2 oz Color B.
Needles: Single point No. 10.

Using No. 10 needles, cast on 50 (62-74) sts *with*

color A. Work in p 2, k 2 for 3 rows.

Row 4:   K 2, *p 1, yo, k 2 tog, k 1, rep from * across row. This is the right side.

Row 5:   P 2, k 2 across and continue this way in ribbing through row 9.

Row 10: *With color B,* start to k. Continue in garter st until there are 16 ridges. End facing a right side row.

With color A: K the next row. Then start to rib p 2, k 2 across. Continue for 4 more rows. Work a yo row like row 4 at the beg. Continue to rib 2 more rows. Then bind off in ribbing.

Fold one short end in half and sew. Crochet a cord in chain st about 7 feet long. Lace the boot. Make pom-poms. Sew pom-poms to the cord.

Watch Hat (see next page)

Make one especially for everyone!...

Watch Cap

A fun little favorite (previous page) that's also known as a pea hat. Cute in striped or solid colors, it makes a warm and kicky hat for outdoor fun. We've given two yarn variation patterns.

Yarn: Worsted Weight 4 oz.
Sizes: Child (under 10) and Adult.
Needles: Double point No. 6.

Cast on 84 (100) sts. Divide the sts evenly on 3 needles being careful not to twist them. Join and work in k 2, p 2 rib for 8 ins.

First Dec Round: *K 2 tog, k 1; rep from * around. Continue working in ss for 2 ins. Rep the dec round. Work 1½ ins more and rep the dec round. Work another ½ in. Break yarn leaving a 10 in

length. Thread it in a darning needle and run the needle through the sts on the knitting needles. Draw up tightly and fasten off the top. Attach a pom-pom, tassel or button if desired.

Yarn: Bulky Weight 4 oz.
Needles: Double point No. 9.

Sizing is the same as for the worsted yarn.

Cast on 56 (68) sts. Follow the directions for the worsted weight yarn.

For those knitters who do not like to knit on circular or dp needles, these caps may be knitted on straight needles. Simply work back and forth on single point needles. At the end leave a length of yarn long enough to sew the back seam as well as fasten off the top. As you can see, the model was done with colored stripes. Add them any place you like and as many as you like. Sew in any dangling ends when you finish the hat.

Be a Knit Whiz...

Goodbye ply

For many years, knitting yarn thickness was designated by the number of plies it had.

Today, "ply" has no meaning as far as thickness of yarn or knitting guage is concerned.

In this book, yarns are described by their average stitch gauge—Baby (Fingering) Yarn, 6½-7½ stitches per inch; Sportsweight, 5½-6 stitches per inch; Knitting Worsted Weight, 4½-5 stitches per inch; Bulky, 3-4 stitches per inch; and Extra Bulky, 2-2½ stitches per inch.

To be sure, ask your yarn shop owner for yarn by the gauge

to be knitted for each particular pattern. All the patterns in this book specify the gauge you'll need to work with.

A special thank you

Ruhama wishes to thank the many customers and friends who loaned sweaters made from these patterns, plus those who stepped in to knit garments specially for photos in this book: Ann Pereles, Dee Sherkow, Bob Herold, Mary Ogie Georg, Jane Green, Elaine Roalkvan, Miriam Willenson, Albert Weiner, Mary Becker and Ruth Pluss.